W9-BIC-729

I confess, I've never been eager to study books like Leviticus. That is until I began reading *7 Feasts* by Erin Davis. I imagine I'm not alone; there are likely parts of the Bible that you gravitate toward, too. As Davis explains in this study, fragmented Bible reading leaves us with an incomplete picture of God. As I read *7 Feasts* I found myself excited, convicted, grateful, eager to know more and, ultimately worshiping Jesus. *7 Feasts* helped me love God with my heart and my mind. You'll be glad you grabbed it.

TRILLIA NEWBELL
Author of the Bible study *If God Is For Us*

Erin Davis is a Bible teacher I find true, studied and deeply in love with the Word. I want to learn from her. She's done the mining to bring us a true gift in *7 Feasts*. Dig in, expectantly.

LISA WHITTLE
Author of *Jesus Over Everything*, Bible teacher, founder of Ministry Strong

Powerful, compelling, and eye-opening! This unique study takes you to rare and unexpected places in Scripture. You'll discover the beauty of Jesus through the lens of the Old Testament celebrations and walk away awed by His glory. You will be refreshed and encouraged in new ways as you journey through the pages of this study. We highly recommend it!

KRISTEN CLARK AND BETHANY BEAL
Authors and founders of GirlDefined Ministries

Few things make me happier than introducing women to hidden treasures in the Word of God. And that's exactly why I'm thrilled to tell women about this study! In it, Erin takes you by the hand, skillfully uncovering the glories of Christ in the pages of our Bible we too often avoid. On top of giving you a clearer understanding of God's character through the Old Testament feasts, this study will also teach you valuable Bible study tools for every book of the Bible. Don't miss out on this gem.

KELLY NEEDHAM
Author of *Friend-ish: Reclaiming Real Friendship in a Culture of Confusion*

Erin's *7 Feasts* landed in my inbox just days after I had finished reading Leviticus on my own, and I sped through it, eager to add to my understanding of how it points to Jesus. Erin proved a compassionate and humorous guide as I filled the less-worn pages of my Bible with notes, discovering with awe how these ancient festivals connected to Jesus two thousand years ago and to modern believers today. As twenty-first century Christians, we no longer have to observe these feasts, but we get to study them to grow in our knowledge and love of Jesus—the One who fulfills it all and draws us into God's presence—that we may remember and celebrate Him until we see Him face-to-face.

ASHERITAH CIUCIU
Author of *Unwrapping the Names of Jesus: An Advent Devotional* and *He Is Enough: Living in the Fullness of Jesus (A Study in Colossians)*

Erin, thank you for setting the table for those of us that want to dig in to God's Word. *7 Feasts* will give readers a hermeneutical fork and knife that will help them feed themselves and teach others to study God's Word for themselves as well.

AMY-JO GIRARDIER
Author and Girls Minister

This Bible study is amazing! Take Erin's hand and join her on an exciting journey to passages of Scripture that are quite unpopular. She will help you discover Christ and the gospel in unlikely places. I am sure that your heart will be fueled with hope!

BETSY GOMEZ
Author, blogger, and media supervisor for *Aviva Nuestros Corazones*

In *7 Feasts*, Erin has done a superb job of laying out a thorough and accessible Bible study that brilliantly guides women through a challenging portion of Old Testament Scripture. As a Bible teacher, I am excited to use this study with the women in my local community (and beyond). As an ever-growing student of Scripture, I am eager to add this resource to my library and I am confident that I will revisit this study for many years to come!

PORTIA COLLINS
Host of the *She Shall Be Called* podcast

AN 8-WEEK BIBLE STUDY

7

FEASTS

—

FINDING CHRIST *in the*
SACRED CELEBRATIONS
of the OLD TESTAMENT

ERIN DAVIS

MOODY PUBLISHERS
CHICAGO

Edited by Amanda Cleary Eastep
Interior design: Erik M. Peterson
Cover design: Dean Renninger
Cover illustration of night sky copyright © 2019 by suns07butterfly / Shutterstock (510481276). All rights reserved.
Author photo: Bonnie Hall

All websites and phone numbers listed herein are accurate at the time of publication but may change in the future or cease to exist. The listing of website references and resources does not imply publisher endorsement of the site's entire contents. Groups and organizations are listed for informational purposes, and listing does not imply publisher endorsement of their activities.

Library of Congress Cataloging-in-Publication Data

Names: Davis, Erin, 1980- author.
Title: 7 feasts : finding Christ in the sacred celebrations of the Old
   Testament / Erin Davis.
Description: Chicago : Moody Publishers, 2020. | Includes bibliographical
   references. | Summary: "What's the story behind all those feasts? It's
   hard to know when you read about the Feast of Booths why exactly it
   matters for your life. What in the world is the Feast of Trumpets
   supposed to be teaching you? And, in this case, the text itself doesn't
   tell you. You need a resource, a guide that can help you understand the
   cultural significance and how these feasts relate to the rest of the
   Bible. That's exactly what Erin Davis does in this new Bible study, 7
   Feasts. She'll teach you: the significance of these feasts and why God
   wanted His people to celebrate; how each of them point to Jesus and His
   work in redemption; and why all of this matters for our lives today. You
   will discover that passages you once skimmed over are now rich and
   meaningful in your life today"-- Provided by publisher.
Identifiers: LCCN 2019058697 (print) | LCCN 2019058698 (ebook) | ISBN
   9780802419552 (paperback) | ISBN 9780802498182 (ebook)
Subjects: LCSH: Fasts and feasts in the Bible. | Fasts and feasts in the
   Bible--Typology. | Bible. Leviticus, XXIII--Criticism, interpretation,
   etc. | Bible--Study and teaching.
Classification: LCC BS1199.F35 D38 2020 (print) | LCC BS1199.F35 (ebook)
   | DDC 221.8/3942--dc23
LC record available at https://lccn.loc.gov/2019058697
LC ebook record available at https://lccn.loc.gov/2019058698

Originally delivered by fleets of horse-drawn wagons, the affordable paperbacks from D. L. Moody's publishing house resourced the church and served everyday people. Now, after more than 125 years of publishing and ministry, Moody Publishers' mission remains the same—even if our delivery systems have changed a bit. For more information on other books (and resources) created from a biblical perspective, go to: www.moodypublishers.com or write to:

Moody Publishers
820 N. LaSalle Boulevard
Chicago, IL 60610

3 5 7 9 10 8 6 4 2

Printed in the United States of America

To Meg, Chandra, and Ashley,

A Blessing . . .

May you delight in the Word of God far above lesser pleasures.
May you run to Him first and often.
May Christ be your greatest treasure and His Word be your greatest joy.
And may you hold the banner of Truth high for your generation.

CONTENTS

STUDY INTRODUCTION

I learned to love puzzles from my grandma.

Every time I went to visit her, I found a puzzle in process on a card table in the corner. She started with the edge pieces and then patiently filled in the interior, piece by piece, until a completed image emerged. Whether it was a watercolor portrait of the Eiffel Tower or a vibrant photograph of a deep sea reef, what started out as a pile of jumbled fragments transformed into something more as she patiently interlocked each piece.

Consider this study an invitation to flip over a new piece of the puzzle.

Picture the Bible like a boxed puzzle. Inside are sixty-six pieces that vary in shape and size. Why sixty-six? Open your Bible to the Table of Contents to find out. The Bible is a big book, composed of many smaller books. Put your finger on Genesis and count all the way to Revelation and you'll discover how many exactly. (Sixty-six, of course.)

The Old Testament holds thirty-nine books, beginning with Genesis and concluding with Malachi. This is where we find familiar favorites like the garden of Eden (Gen. 1–3), Noah and the flood (Gen. 6–10), and Jonah and the whale (book of Jonah). It's also where we meet Moses, Esther, David, and Daniel. The Old Testament is older than the New on the timeline of human history, but there is another important distinction that separates these books from everything that comes after them on the pages of God's Word; the Old Testament includes the parts of the Bible that were written *before the birth of Christ.*

Are your eyes starting to roll back into your head right now? Does all of this feel a bit like the first week of school, when you're forced to review all that you've already learned?

Maybe you already knew there were sixty-six books and you're as familiar with the structure of Scripture as I am with my favorite coffee mug. Stick with me. We are heading somewhere. Scout's honor.

The remaining twenty-seven books of the Bible are found in the New Testament. Don't you just love the New Testament? It's where we find the Gospels and Paul's letters, along with practical gems like James and 1 John. My very favorite passages are found in the New Testament. If you could peek at my Bible you'd see books like John, Ephesians, and Revelation well marked.

I bet you have some favorite places in your own Bible. Take a moment and flip through. Where do you see signs of wear? Where does your Bible fall open easily out of habit? Maybe you love the hopeful poetry of the Psalms or the wisdom found in Proverbs. Perhaps you resonate with Paul's conviction in the book of Romans or Peter's righteous reminders in 1 and 2 Peter.

Familiar is good, especially when we're talking about familiarity with God's Word. The more we know the Bible, the more we are sure to love it. Saturating yourself in familiar passages and themes is a profitable habit. *But, the time has come to go off road.*

The purpose of Scripture is . . . drum roll please . . . to reveal who God is. Though God is certainly mysterious, He has chosen to reveal His character clearly through the pages of His Word. Lean in. Listen closely. This is important. *We study our Bibles to know God.*

Back to the puzzle. If God's Word is a sixty-six piece puzzle, and there are parts of it we avoid, the result will be an incomplete picture of God. Even if you know several books of the Bible inside and out, you've only turned over a corner of the picture God chooses to reveal of Himself in His Word.

Only when we commit to becoming lifelong students of God's Word, to patiently flipping over each piece and looking for how it interlocks with the rest of Scripture, do we learn how to see the whole picture.

Enter the Seven Feasts.

The Seven Feasts of Israel are found in Leviticus 23. As we spend the next eight weeks exploring each feast, we'll find so much more than antiquated rules and rituals. The feasts were established as constant object lessons on the character and faithfulness of God. By looking closely at this piece of the puzzle, we gain new glimpses of His character.

Maybe you've never looked at the Seven Feasts before, or perhaps you've never seen them as anything more than an out-of-date list of celebrations from a foreign culture in a hard-to-read book.

Trust me. They are so much more.

When our time together is over, and you write your final notes on the last page of this study, I want this idea to be firmly fixed in your hearts: *every piece of the puzzle of God's Word matters because all of God's Word shows us who God is.* The picture on the box of this puzzle is more beautiful, more hopeful, and more life-changing than we can fully grasp.

But let's try!

Just like my grandmother's approach when assembling a puzzle, we will start with what we know. When I think about what I know about God's Word, these truths come to mind:

I know the Bible is God-breathed (2 Tim. 3:16).

I know it matters.

I know there's a lot I don't know.

I know God's Word has completely transformed me.

Before you jump in fully to the pages of this study and dig around in the box looking for the pieces that reveal the feasts, let's start with what you know. What do you know to be true about the Word of God? *Write whatever comes to mind in the space below.*

I'm not writing to you as an expert theologian who has everything about the feasts figured out. Like you, I simply want to know Jesus better. The great quest of my life is to love Him more and more.

So, brew yourself a cup of something delicious. Throw your hair back into a ponytail, and pull up a chair. I can't wait to spend the next eight weeks with you, assembling this puzzle, one piece at a time.

Rooting for you!

Erin

The Cure for Spiritual Amnesia

Welcome to Week One! I hope you have that first-day-of-school feeling of excitement mixed with a touch of nervousness. I do. I've spent months praying for the women who would pick up this study. *You, friend, are a dream come true.*

Each week is divided into five daily studies. Take them a day at a time, or clump a few together. Find a pace that works well for you. Just don't try to cram them all in fifteen minutes before you're supposed to be at your women's Bible study, deal? I've been there and done that. If racing through a study is your goal, that approach might work. But my hope is that we might be *transformed* by the pages of God's Word. That requires diligence. *Whoever is doing the work is doing the learning.* The more we give this study our focused attention in the weeks ahead, God's Word will transform us.

Here are some tools that can help along the way:

- **A study Bible.** We'll be focusing on a portion of Scripture where time-
  lines and cultural references might feel a little clunky. A good study Bible
  keeps helpful insights nearby.

- **A good pen.** Our Bibles aren't meant to be preserved for a future museum
  display. They are meant to be *used*! Writing in your Bible helps you engage
  with the text you are reading. Circle repeated phrases, write questions and
  prayers in the margins, underline the words of God. If you want to do it in
  style, use my favorite pens, Papermate Flairs. Swoon!

- **Other women.** Other women bring a richness to the study of God's
  Word that we can't find anywhere else. Ask a friend or two to go through
  this study with you or participate in a larger group through your church.
  I've included group discussion questions after each chapter to make it easy
  and you can find a more detailed group guide at erindavis.org.

This week, we'll see that we're all prone to forget the character of God. Instead of
letting us wander in that dazed state, God has a plan to remind us who He is. May
you find your heart tethered more closely to His this week.

HERMENWHATICS?

BIG IDEA: *We can handle God's Word "rightly."*

READ PSALM 119:9–16

If I were to place all of the weapons that exist in the Davis household into a single pile, you might be able to see it from space. I am the mother of four boys. And boys being boys, they are big fans of the instruments of war. We have NERF guns galore, foam bullets in spades, and pocket knives in every pocket, drawer, and hidey hole.

As each boy nears double digits, their daddy teaches them how to whittle. It's a supervised way to learn how to handle a sharp blade rightly. Every boy has needed a bandage or two along the way, but by God's grace, there are still forty little boy fingers in my house.

Why do I tell you all of that? In part, because I love to talk about my boys. (Wanna see a picture?) But more importantly, because as we open God's Word together, I want us to remember that it's a sword.

Consider Paul's words found in Ephesians 6:16–17, "In all circumstances take up the shield of faith, with which you can extinguish all the flaming darts of the evil one; and take the helmet of salvation, and the sword of the Spirit, which is the word of God."

We're going to make a habit of reading Scripture slowly and intentionally in this study. It takes focus to click the pieces of the puzzle together. Let's start now.

Go back and reread Ephesians 6:16–17. How is the Word of God described?

The author of Hebrews gives us a similar description. Write out Hebrews 4:12 below.

Again, we see sword language here. A sword may be an antiquated weapon, but God's Word isn't getting dull displayed on a shelf. *The Bible is sharp and ready for battle.*

Why do you think the writer of this passage describes God's Word in this way?

Yes, the Bible is a comfort, reminding us we can hope in God's care.

True, it is a teacher, revealing the mysteries of who God is.

It certainly is a guide, teaching us how to live.

But make no mistake, it is also a weapon, cutting away at the parts of us that do not bear the image of God.

That's why we find this important warning embedded in 2 Timothy 2:15: "Do your best to present yourself to God as one approved, a worker who has no need to be ashamed, rightly handling the word of truth."

Circle the word that describes how we are to handle the Word of God.

Paul's warning to handle God's Word "rightly" reminds us that it's possible to handle it wrongly. As imperfect sinners with limited knowledge and understanding, it's possible to misunderstand or misapply the perfect Word of God.

HERMENWHATICS?

As I study the Bible, I've found the Rules of Hermeneutics to be so helpful. Hermeneutics is a fancy word for application. These are guidelines for how we rightly apply (or handle) God's Word.

Scholars have spent endless hours and reservoirs of ink writing about these rules. Since I'm not a scholar, and my words are limited, here's a crash course. Take a moment to write down any thoughts or questions you have about each rule.

Rule #1: We let Scripture interpret Scripture.

It is essential for us to interpret a passage in light of what the rest of Scripture says on the topic. A correct interpretation is always consistent with the rest of Scripture.

Thoughts: Questions:

Rule #2: We pay close attention to context.

Every word in the Bible is part of a verse.
Every verse is part of a paragraph.
Every paragraph is part of a book.
Every book is part of the whole of Scripture.

No verse of Scripture should be divorced from the verses around it.

We will spend the next eight weeks hyperfocused on one chapter in one book in the Bible, but the goal is to connect what we find in Leviticus 23 with what we find in the rest of God's Word.

Thoughts: Questions:

Rule #3: Pause to consider what type of book or passage you're reading.

Here are some broad categories that can be used to help us understand the context of most Scripture passages:

1) Epistles or Letters
2) Gospels
3) Parables
4) Eschatology
5) Apocalyptic
6) Law
7) Historical Narrative
8) Hebrew Poetry
9) Prophecy
10) Wisdom

Taking a moment to pause and consider what type of writing we're reading in Scripture helps us rightly apply God's Word in our lives.

Let's practice.

READ ECCLESIASTES 7:1-3

Write the reference next to the category it falls under in the list above.

READ LUKE 15:3-7

Write the reference next to the category it falls under in the list above.

Thoughts: Questions:

Rule #4: Try to discern the writer's intentions when he wrote the text.

A passage cannot mean something to us today that it was never intended to mean to the original audience.

The Bible is unique in its timelessness. In this study, we will read words written centuries ago that still apply to us, and yet, they were not originally written just for us. We can grow in rightly handling the Word by training ourselves to consider the original hearers of each text.

Thoughts: Questions:

Rule #5: Keep it simple.

The Bible is not a book of riddles to be solved. God is not a God of confusion, but of clarity (1 Cor. 14:33). He has not spoken in order to conceal, but to be understood and known (Isa. 48:6; Jer. 33:3).

When we open God's Word, it is the plain meaning of the text we are seeking to understand.

Let's practice.

READ MARK 4:1-9

We could go round and round on this passage if we chose to. We could debate hidden meanings and possible applications; instead, let's keep it simple.

What is Christ teaching us in this verse?

In this case, we have the gift of Christ's explanation of the parable.

READ MARK 4:10-20

How does your understanding of the parable match up to Christ's? Is your explanation more simple or more complex than His?

There are certainly parts of Scripture that are complex and impossible to reduce to a simplistic command. Thank goodness we have the Holy Spirit to help us as we read! But generally, it is wise to approach the Bible looking for the simplest explanation of what is being revealed.

Thoughts: Questions:

Rule #6: Always take a God-centered approach.

Avoid looking at Scripture primarily to better understand yourself or correct your actions. Ask yourself, "What does this show me about God?" before you ask, "What does this tell me about me?" or "What should I do?" *Right application of Scripture is only ever an outflow of right understanding of who God is.*

In order of importance, this is rule #1, but I've placed it here, so we can linger on this thought for a moment.

As women, we are hardwired to want to be pleasing. It is one of the ways we bear the image of God.

We want to be good daughters, good wives, good mothers, good friends, good employees, and good Christ followers. Often we open our Bible with that goal, however subconsciously, in mind. We're looking for ways to make adjustments in order to be better women. God is gracious to transform us through His Word. He will reshape you as you read, but the Bible is not primarily a self-help guide. Here is a truth I must remind myself of often:

The Bible is not a book about you. The Bible is a book about Jesus.

This shift is important. We will not open the Bible together in these weeks searching for a clearer view of ourselves. We will open the Bible searching for a clearer, bigger, more awe-inspiring view of God. As we do, we will be changed. *We are better able to bear the image of God when we better understand the character of God.*

Consider your own personal approach to Scripture. Is there evidence that you tend to take a God-centered approach, opening your Bible primarily to see God? Or a me-centered approach, opening your Bible to primarily see yourself? How can you tell?

Is there evidence of a hybrid approach, sometimes searching for God and sometimes searching for self in the pages of your Bible? How can you tell?

Like my little boys learning to whittle, we just practiced handling the Word of God in a way that guards, protects, and reshapes our hearts. We will stay within these guardrails as we consider the Seven Feasts. I'm asking the Lord to remind you of them well beyond the weeks of this study.

This is my prayer for you:

> *Jesus, thank You for the gift of Your Word. Grow our hunger for it and teach us to open it looking for You. Lord, train every woman who works through this study to be a spiritual samurai, rightly wielding the Word of Truth in their lives and in the culture around them. Amen.*

What are you asking the Lord to do in your life through this study? Write out your prayer below.

RULES FOR WANDERING

BIG IDEA: *God's Law works like guardrails to protect us as we wander.*

READ EXODUS 24

I've put all of my babies to sleep with my favorite hymn, "Come, Thou Fount of Every Blessing." It's a prayer I sing over their lives. I sing some of its words over your life too.

Come, thou Fount of every blessing,
tune my heart to sing thy grace;
streams of mercy, never ceasing,
call for songs of loudest praise.
Teach me some melodious sonnet,
sung by flaming tongues above.
Praise the mount I'm fixed upon it
mount of God's redeeming love.

This verse always puts a lump in my throat.

Oh, to grace how great a debtor
daily I'm constrained to be!
Let thy goodness, like a fetter,
bind my wandering heart to thee:

prone to wander, Lord, I feel it,
prone to leave the God I love;
here's my heart, O take and seal it;
seal it for thy courts above.[1]

I've chosen this hymn over other lullabies because my boys have my DNA. They also share the DNA of their foreparents, Adam and Eve. Which means, like me (like all of us) they are sinners, prone to wander from the God they love.

Church history holds a precious story of Robert Robinson, the author of this eighteenth-century hymn. Though the story is unconfirmed, I've often heard the tale of Robert riding in a stagecoach years after he came to Christ. A woman in the coach asked him his thoughts on the hymn she was humming. Robert reportedly replied, "Madam, I am the poor unhappy man who wrote that hymn many years ago, and I would give a thousand worlds, if I had them, to enjoy the feelings I had then."[2]

I can't presume to know what Robert was feeling in that moment. But I know what I've felt in the more than twenty years I've been walking with Christ. There have been times when I've felt:

- squashed by my own sin
- defeated by my inability to be holy as God is holy
- frustrated at how slow the sanctification process is
- tempted to question the goodness of God in the midst of difficult circumstances
- wandering from the wonder of loving God and knowing His Word . . .

We're all prone to wander, aren't we? Our sinful hearts are prone to wander from God's law. We are prone to forget His precious promises. We tend to prioritize our way over God's way.

Take a moment to pray. Ask the Holy Spirit to show you how you are prone to wander. Write down anything that comes to mind.

If you've ever felt, like Robert may have, like you are the only child of God with a wandering heart, *you'll love the book of Leviticus. It is a book for wanderers.*

Before we get there, we need to backtrack to the book of Exodus. (Remember, every piece of the puzzle connects to the other pieces). Let's quickly see how the people of Israel found themselves wandering.

Look up the Exodus passages below. Write down the events recorded in each passage. I've filled in a few for you.

Exodus 1:8–14

- New king in Egypt
- Threatened by the Israelites
- Set taskmasters over the Israelites
- God's people built cities for Pharaoh
- God's people multiplied
- Israelites enslaved

Exodus 2:23–25

Exodus 3:7–12

Exodus 12:29–32

- The LORD strikes down all the firstborn in Egypt
- A great cry in Egypt
- Pharaoh summons Moses, lets the Israelites go

Exodus 12:50–51

According to Exodus 12:40–41, how many years of history did we just cover?

We'll circle back to some of the details we missed in the weeks ahead, but for now, let's focus on the major milestones.

What problems were God's people facing?

How did God intervene? What did He promise them?

Wouldn't it be great if this is how this story ended? The people of God experienced miraculous deliverance, then peacefully walked into the Promised Land. Hooray. Pass the popcorn.

But we're all prone to wander, prone to leave the God we love. The Israelites wandered from one form of captivity to another. They simply swapped taskmasters from Pharaoh to unbelief, rebellion, and discontentment.

According to Exodus 16:35, it took _____ for the Israelites to get to the Promised Land of Canaan.

That's a lot of wandering. Which brings us to the book of Leviticus. Consider writing the words "Rules for wandering" next to the Leviticus heading in your Bible. Though a complicated book, at its core it is a guide to help God's people wander in the wilderness. It lists the rules to keep the nation of Israel tethered to Him because of their tendency to stray.

READ LEVITICUS 27:34

Who, specifically, did God reveal the Levitical laws to? Where were they handed down? Who are they for?

If the headline of Exodus 24 is about the Mosaic covenant, Leviticus is the fine print. Yes, it is a book of laws and rituals, but let's think of them instead like guardrails given by a loving Father. Despite their chronic rebellion, the book of Leviticus is proof that God cares for His people and provides boundaries for our protection. My friend Rabbi Lane Steinger[3] (you'll hear more from him throughout this study) says that he prefers not to call the Torah (the first five books of the Old Testament, including Leviticus) the law, but "teaching" or "instruction." Instead of calling the specific rules listed in Leviticus "commands" or "laws," he focuses on the Hebrew meaning of the word as it relates to providing direction. For example, "*Torah*, the common Hebrew word for law, comes from a Hebrew word meaning to *point out* or *direct*."[4] Like a loving parent who communicates and enforces rules for their child's protection, Leviticus outlines the "rules" or "instructions" needed for God's people to thrive.

Next to each of the following passages, write down <u>why</u> God asks His people to obey His law.

Joshua 1:8

1 Kings 2:2–4

Ezekiel 20:19–20

God's law is for our good. Leviticus isn't just a book of rules arbitrarily handed down by a detached authority. They are opportunities to learn how to live, given to us by our patient Teacher. This paradigm shift matters, because it speaks to the heart of God.

To wrap up today's study, write out the final verse below of "Come, Thou Fount of Every Blessing" (shared earlier) as your own prayer today.

WEEK 1 | DAY 3

THE CURE FOR SPIRITUAL AMNESIA

BIG IDEA: *God's Word cures our spiritual amnesia.*

READ LEVITICUS 23:1–2

Imagine waking up tomorrow with a mind full of blank memories. You can't recall who your parents are, where you live, or where you are employed. It happened to Jody Roberts.

In 1985, a 26-year-old crime reporter at the Tacoma News Tribune named Jody Roberts disappeared. Though she left no trace, her family suspected foul play. Five days after Jody vanished, a young woman wearing a University of Denver sweatshirt walked out of a suburban Denver shopping mall and panicked because she could not remember who she was. Doctors tried to help her, but could not restore her memory. With no memories of her past to orient her, she requested a new social security number, adopted the name Jane Dee, enrolled in college, and tried to move on.

Twelve years later authorities discovered Jody living as Jane in Alaska, now as a married mother of four. She had no memory of her life in the lower 48, but she agreed to reunite with the parents she forgot.[5]

She still goes by Jane Dee. The memories of her previous life have never returned.

Amnesia like Jane's impacts less than three percent of the population,[6] but there is another form of amnesia that affects us all. I call it "spiritual amnesia." The nation of Israel, described in Exodus, makes the perfect case study for this condition.

Scripture records many moments when the people of God—not unlike Jody panicking at a Colorado shopping mall—frantically forgot all God had done for them.

Fill in the chart below to record Israel's history of spiritual amnesia.

WHAT WAS THEIR COMPLAINT?	WHAT DID THEY FORGET?
Exodus 14:10–12	Exodus 12:30–32
Exodus 16:1–3	Exodus 1:13–14
Exodus 17:1–2	Exodus 15:22–25
Numbers 11:1–6	Exodus 3:7–12
Numbers 14:1–4	Exodus 6:2–8

Do you ever read these accounts of the people of Israel and find yourself shaking your head in frustration?

- These are the children God promised to Abraham. (Gen. 22:17)
- These are the people who saw the tablets of stone on which God carved the Ten Commandments with His own finger. (Ex. 31:18)
- These are the ones who cried out for a deliverer and enjoyed the supernatural protection of God as Moses ushered in twelve terrible plagues. (Ex. 7–12)

Their feet walked across the Red Sea on dry ground, their bellies had been filled with manna that rained down from heaven, and their parched lips had been quenched by water God supernaturally squeezed from a stone (Ex. 17:1–7).

Surely, these memories were seared into their hearts. Surely, these stories were told and retold around every campfire. Surely, surely their faith was unshakeable. Instead, we find them to be a forgetful bunch, chronically drawing a blank about the faithfulness of God.

If we read these verses and think we are different in this way, we've lost track of why these stories are in the Bible in the first place.

READ ROMANS 15:4 BELOW.

"For whatever was written in former days was written for our instruction, that through endurance and through the encouragement of the Scriptures we might have hope."

Now write that same verse here to cement it in your own heart and mind:

Let's park here a while, letting our hearts marinate in this important revelation about why the ancient stories are worth paying attention to.

"For whatever was written in former days . . ."

To better grasp this phrase, let's zoom out and consider the bigger puzzle.

Flip back a few pages to Romans 1:1, followed by verse 7. Who wrote the book of Romans? Who did he write this book to?

Right out of the gate we know that Paul is writing this letter to non-Jews, followers of Jesus living in Rome.

Let's widen the lens a little more.

READ GALATIANS 1:15–16

According to this passage, who was Paul called to preach to? (Be specific.)

Though Paul was a devout Jew before his conversion, after meeting Christ, he dedicated his life to preaching the gospel to non-Jews (a.k.a. Gentiles).

Surely the Gentiles in Paul's day were asking, "Why does Scripture matter to us?" The Old Testament was, after all, written by Israelites, for Israelites.

Much of the book of Romans is dedicated to addressing the role of the law (Old Testament) in the life of the New Testament Gentile believer (that's us!). It can serve as our guide as we ask the same question as believers in Paul's day: *Why do the stories of the nation of Israel from thousands of years ago matter to us today?*

Let's head back to Romans 15:4: "For whatever was written in former days *was written for our instruction . . .*"

According to that verse, why was the desert wandering of God's people recorded?

What is Scripture teaching us about? (Hint: What is the purpose of Scripture?)

"For whatever was written in former days was written for our instruction, *that through endurance and through the encouragement of the Scriptures . . .*"

The Bible is an enduring book. What does 1 Peter 1:25 tell us about how long God's Word will last? Write the verse here.

The Bible is also an encouraging book. Let's finish Romans 15:4 to see why.

"For whatever was written in former days was written for our instruction, that through endurance and through the encouragement of the Scriptures *we might have hope.*"

In revealing who God is, the Bible shows us the only source of true hope. The stories of the wandering, forgetful Israelites aren't ultimately about *them.* They're about *Him.* When we humble ourselves and see how much our sinful hearts are prone to spiritual amnesia, we see how much hope is truly found in the faithfulness of God.

Write out Psalm 103:2 below.

Yes, David, the greatest human king of the nation of Israel . . . David, the giant slayer . . . David, the "man after God's own heart" had spiritual amnesia too. So he gave himself this advice, "Bless the LORD, O my soul, and forget not all his benefits."

In other words, praise and remember. Praise and remember. Praise and remember.

Let's head back to Leviticus 23:1–2. The feasts are not just days on the calendar, they are an invitation to a forgetful people, given by a faithful God, *to praise and remember.* Praise and remember.

We all have spiritual amnesia, but there is a cure. "Bless the LORD, O my soul, and forget not all his benefits" (Ps. 103:2).

Below make a list of the worries and fears that weigh you down today. Here is a peek at my list:

- I worry about the health of my aging parents.
- I have fears about the cultural darkness that seems to be growing.
- I worry that I won't get everything that is needed done today and I will disappoint God and others.

Write your burdens in the chart that follows. Next to each worry or fear on your list, list a quality or characteristic of God, or a time when He has come through for you, to remind you of His faithfulness.

Here are some qualities of God that give me specific comfort:

- God is attentive to our needs.
- God is sovereign over all things.
- God's love for me is everlasting.

Your turn.

MY BURDENS	GOD'S FAITHFULNESS

DIVINE RHYTHMS

BIG IDEA: *God has established rhythms to help us turn toward Him.*

READ GENESIS 1

I like to have a plan. I like to know the plan. I like to write the plan in pretty colors in my day planner.

How about you? When it comes to your calendar, how would you rate yourself on the scale below?

Wanna see my spreadsheet?   I make plans in pencil   Plan? What plan?

| 1 | 2 | 3 | 4 | 5 | 6 | 7 | 8 | 9 | 10 |

Whether you are a planner to a T or a fly-by-the-seat-of-your-pants kinda girl, your life has rhythms. Daily rhythms feed into monthly rhythms, which flow into yearly rhythms, which ultimately become the cadence of our lives.

Open your Bible to Genesis 1. We're going to walk through the creation of the world, looking for rhythms.

First things first: "In the beginning, God created the heavens and the earth" (v. 1).

READ GENESIS 1:2

Describe what's happening in this verse.

Don't worry if you struggle to come up with something to write. Not much was happening. The Spirit of God was hovering, but the earth was without form and void. Void of what? Among other things, it was void of *rhythms*.

The sun wasn't rising in the east each morning and setting in the west each evening. The tide wasn't coming in and going out. People weren't sipping their morning cup of coffee or tucking their children into bed.

What other creation rhythms can you think of? Make a list below.

As we keep reading, we hear a drumbeat start. The rhythms of life are about to begin.

Day 1
READ VV. 3–5
What did God say?

What did God make?

How did creation respond?

Day 2
READ VV. 6–8
What did God say?

What did God make?

How did creation respond?

Day 3
READ VV. 9–13
What did God say?

What did God make?

How did creation respond?

Day 4
READ VV. 14–19
What did God say?

What did God make?

How did creation respond?

Day 5
READ VV. 20–23
What did God say?

What did God make?

How did creation respond?

Day 6
READ VV. 24–31
What did God say?

What did God make?

How did creation respond?

Life on planet earth has always had a pattern. God speaks. Creation responds. The sun sets. The sun rises. Repeat.

Take a moment to consider your own rhythms. What does a typical day look like? A typical month? A typical year?

At the dawn of creation God gave us life. He gave us light, and food, and zebras, and strawberries . . . He also gave us *the calendar*, a blueprint for the daily rhythms of our lives.

Perhaps you've never stopped to consider why we have a seven-day week, and not a two-day week or a two-hundred day week. (Though some weeks feel that long). Right here, on the first pages of our Bibles we see God establishing this rhythm.

How many days did He create? How many days did He rest?

Other calendar patterns can be found in the world He created.

> **Years** are marked by the passage of seasons. Days lengthen and then shorten, and then lengthen again.

> **Months** are marked by the cycles of the moon. Astronomers recognize four primary moon phases: new moon, first quarter moon, full moon, and last quarter moon. Don't worry, there won't be a quiz, but I'm about to give us the one and only math equation in this study. Calculators encouraged!

Creation follows the pattern God established here in Genesis.

How many days are in the average month? _____

Divide the number of days in the average month by the four phases of the moon. What's the nearest whole number? _____

Seven!

A seven-day week is built into the framework of existence. It's always been a part of God's plan.

The drumbeat established at creation continues through the Jewish calendar outlined in Leviticus 23. The Seven Feasts mirror the seven days of creation. Again, God speaks and creation responds.

One of the greatest gifts the Seven Feasts can give us is attention to the rhythms of our lives. God was writing in the planners of His people to help them remember who He is. He was establishing rhythms of work, rest, and worship to keep them tethered to Him, even as they wandered.

As New Testament Christians, we're not bound to a strict observance of the Seven Feasts, but if we let them, the feasts will reshape our rhythms to shift our focus toward Him. The feasts can help us pay attention to, and participate in the other rhythms God has established for His people.

Let me show you. Look up Luke 22:14–23. What rhythm was Christ establishing?

What was He helping us remember?

From creation, to Leviticus, to the Gospels (and beyond) God has always established rhythms to help us seek Him. He set the calendar in the sky. He modeled a pattern of work and rest for us to follow. He gave us rituals to help us remember who He is.

As you close this day's study, consider your lists of daily, monthly, and annual rhythms.

- Do you see patterns that point you to Jesus often?
- Is He the focus of your days, your weeks, your years?
- Do your rhythms need adjustment to remind you of who He is more?

CHANGE THE PATTERN

BIG IDEA: *God invites us to regularly change the pattern of our lives.*

READ LEVITICUS 23:1–3

If you passed middle school civics, I bet you can recite the preamble to the U.S. Constitution. Go ahead, try.

We the People . . .

A preamble is just what it sounds like. It's the words that come before the main idea, the "pre" before the "amble."

Leviticus 23:1–3 gives us the preamble to the Seven Feasts. These verses set the stage for the rest of the feasts.

First, God gives Moses the assignment to announce the feasts to His people, but then He seems to take a detour. Instead of announcing a feast, He reminds Israel of the importance of the Sabbath.

Sabbath is a relatively new concept for God's people at this point. They had moved from being slaves, bound to work for their masters all day, every day, to being free. When God handed down the Ten Commandments at Mount Sinai, Sabbath became a new rhythm for the free people of God.

Read Exodus 20:2–17 and divide the commandments into the two categories below.

RELATIONSHIP WITH GOD	RELATIONSHIP WITH OTHERS

Where did you put the fourth commandment, "remember the Sabbath day, to keep it holy"? Explain.

While some of the commandments may fit easily into one category or another, the command to observe the Sabbath doesn't fit by design. To understand why, let's define the type of Sabbath God was commanding His people to observe.

Write out Exodus 20:8–11. God gives us both the what and the why of Sabbath in these verses.

What was He commanding His people to do (or not do?)

Why was He commanding them to do it?

Sabbath is not a list of tasks to complete or sins to avoid. Instead, it is an invitation to change the pattern, to take a break from creating and building and working and striving.

What does Isaiah 40:28 tell us?

Since God did not rest on the seventh day because He was tired, there must be more value to a day of rest than a chance to catch up on some Z's. *The Sabbath is not about what we do with our hands, it's about what we do with our hearts.*

READ MARK 2:23-28

Go back through the passage and circle every instance of the word "Sabbath."

Revisit verse 23. What did the disciples do that offended the Pharisees?

Underline verse 27. Write out verse 28.

The Pharisees looked at the Sabbath as a list of do's or don'ts. Jesus takes time to remind them of two important truths.

1. God is in charge. He gets to decide what Sabbath means.

2. Sabbath is a gift God gives to us, not a hoop we jump through for Him.

We'll see the command to Sabbath repeated in four of the Seven Feasts. As we explore the feasts, we'll get a clearer picture of exactly what Sabbath involved for the Israelites as they wandered and what it can look like for us today.

For now, know that the Sabbath is a divine invitation to change the pattern. Think back to creation.

Day 1: God created

Day 2: God created

Day 3: God created

Day 4: God created

Day 5: God created

Day 6: God created

Day 7: **God changed the pattern.**

The Seven Feasts and the Sabbath are examples of ways God invites His people to change the pattern—to look up from our work and rest in His work; to stop gazing at ourselves and to gaze at Him instead; to unclench our fists and open our hands for the gifts He has for His children.

With this in mind, why do you think the command to Sabbath doesn't fit easily into either the category of our relationship with God or our relationship with others?

Our willingness to Sabbath impacts every corner of our lives, our work, our relationship with God, our relationship with others . . . everything! If we cannot stop and rest, we cannot focus on all that God has done. If we never change the pattern, our hearts will never turn toward God.

I need to end this day of study with a confession: I don't Sabbath well. I am a firstborn, type A achiever. I highly value getting things done. Since I am the mother of four small boys on a busy farm, there is *always* work to do. Left to my own devices, I will not change the pattern until my mind and body hit a brick wall, leading to discouragement, despair, and irritability. God's command to Sabbath produces the dual results of relief and anxiety in me; I desperately want to rest from my toil while simultaneously worrying that if I do, the laundry pile will reach cruising altitude.

This is why I need God's Word so much! It is constantly reshaping my priorities and shifting my focus. It is a daily invitation to surrender my plans for *my days, my weeks, my years* in favor of the better portion God has for me.

The Seven Feasts and the command to Sabbath are singing in concert with all of Scripture. This is their refrain, "All the ends of the earth shall remember and turn to the Lord, and all the families of the nations shall worship before you" (Ps. 22:27).

Jesus, we invite you to change the pattern of our lives, so that we can see you more clearly.

Amen?

Wrap up today's study, by prayerfully taking the assessment below, asking the Lord to show you how you can change the pattern to turn toward Him more often.

AM I WILLING TO CHANGE THE PATTERN?

1 = *yes, absolutely*   **5** = *sometimes/maybe*   **10** = *no, never*

Do I regularly practice Sabbath?

1   2   3   4   5   6   7   8   9   10

Is my fatigue based on temporary circumstances (vs. a chronic, ongoing state of being)?

1   2   3   4   5   6   7   8   9   10

Do I worry that if I take a break from my to-do list I'll never catch up?

1   2   3   4   5   6   7   8   9   10

As I look at the week ahead, do I see scheduled pockets to focus on the Lord?

1   2   3   4   5   6   7   8   9   10

Am I comfortable with white space on my calendar (times when there is nothing scheduled)?

1   2   3   4   5   6   7   8   9   10

3 QUESTIONS FOR GROUP STUDY

Our understanding of God's Word is deepened when we read and discuss the Bible with others. But let's face it, group discussion can be . . . awkward. I've tried many different methods to encourage fruitful Bible study with varying results, but for many years have relied heavily on a three questions method. These three simple questions help us ask the right questions of Scripture in the right order. I hope they will lead to fruitful (not awkward) conversations around your dinner table, in your living rooms, and in the classrooms at your church. Apply them to the entire week, or use them to unpack each day of study.

PS: If you're a teacher who prefers more extensive teaching helps, check out the *7 Feasts* resources at ErinDavis.org.

1. What does this tell us about God?

2. What does this tell us about us?

3. How should we respond?

The Passover

In his camel hair tunic in the middle of his locust and wild honey cleanse (Matt. 3:4), John the Baptist stood on the banks of the Jordan River and proclaimed, "Behold, the Lamb of God, who takes away the sin of the world!" (John 1:29).

If we race past John's statement, we miss something significant. John wasn't unique because of his fashion sense and food choices. He was unique because he was among the very few who recognized the tipping point when it happened. He knew that all of history was about to shift.

Before Christ performed a single miracle . . .
Before Jesus predicted His own death and resurrection . . .
Before Jesus hung on a cross between two criminals . . .

John made a bold prophecy; *recognizing Jesus as the spotless Lamb who would be sacrificed for the sins of the world.* John was pointing forward to the coming cross and backward to one of the Seven Feasts.

John's language of sacrifice can be traced all the way back to Exodus 12 when the people of Israel were told the gospel story as they fled captivity in Egypt. This week we'll explore the Passover. As you complete each day of study, may your heart be captivated by the realization that this ancient celebration points forward to Jesus, *the Lamb of God.*

ENSLAVED!

BIG IDEA: *Israel's enslavement in Egypt is a picture of our slavery to sin.*

READ EXODUS 1

I celebrated my twentieth spiritual birthday with back sweat and blisters.

I was fifteen years old when I surrendered my life to Christ on a hot summer night at camp. As the twentieth anniversary of that decision approached, I knew I wanted to celebrate in a big way. I vowed to walk twenty miles in an attempt to raise $20,000 to give away to the ministries that had most impacted my relationship with Christ.

It was July (a.k.a. hot) in Missouri (a.k.a. humid) and just in case you're wondering, walking stops being fun somewhere around mile number eleven (a.k.a. out of shape).

Why did I give up a Saturday in my air-conditioned home to pound the pavement in the heat? I wanted to remember—strike that—I needed to remember that, before Christ, I was enslaved to the terrible taskmasters of sin and death. My spiritual amnesia makes it so easy to forget all that He delivered me from.

I also needed the jarring, physical reminder that there are people around me who are still in chains. They are my friends and family, my neighbors and coworkers, the other moms in the car line and the other shoppers in the checkout line . . . the ones who don't have a moment of freedom to celebrate because they don't yet know Christ, the Deliverer.

In Exodus 1, we see Israel become a shackled nation. As we explore the Passover together this week, we will see that this feast was (like my long hot walk) a planned celebration of their liberation. Let's trace their steps to see how Israel got to Egypt in the first place.

READ GENESIS 15:18–21

What gift did God give Abram?

Ever wonder why the land Israel fled to is called the "Promised Land?" The answer is found right here in these verses. This is land that God *promised* Abraham when He commissioned him as the father of the nation.

Israel's creation story began with abundant land and generous promises. Abraham remained a free man in the Promised Land until his death (Gen. 25:7–11). His family remained in that land until a series of providential events surrounding Abraham's great-grandson, Joseph.

Write down what you already know about Joseph's story.

According to Genesis 30:1, 22–24, who were Joseph's parents?

According to Genesis 37:18–28, how did Joseph become separated from his family?

What country did his captors take him to (v. 28)?

Eventually Joseph's brothers and their families (the baby nation of Israel) joined him in Egypt and a fruitful multiplication began. We're up to speed. Let's turn our attention to Exodus 1.

READ EXODUS 1:1–16

Why was Pharaoh threatened by Israel (v. 10)?

How did the citizens of Egypt feel about the Israelite refugees within their borders (v. 12)?

What course of action did the Egyptians eventually take against the Israelites (vv. 13–14)?

Write down the command of Pharaoh recorded in Exodus 1:16.

Oppressed by an evil ruler, and shackled to patterns they could not escape from, the beloved children of God were forced to live under the long, dark shadow of fear and death.

Friend, I hope you have a lump in your throat. I see us in every person enslaved under Pharaoh's tyranny. *Apart from Christ, we're all enslaved.* Satan is a powerful enemy, bent on our oppression, and sin is our terrible taskmaster.

Record Jesus' words found in John 8:34.

Have you ever sinned? Circle yes *or* no.

Your answer is yes. My answer is yes. The honest answer of every human must be yes. We're all sinners. Jesus shows us the clear result of our sin nature in a single sentence. Without His redemptive work, and the power of the Holy Spirit in our lives, *we are slaves to sin, shackled to the power of sin in our lives.*

How has sin led to enslavement in your own life?

In the lives of the people you love most?

That bad news comes with worse news.

"For the wages of sin is death, but the free gift of God is eternal life in Christ Jesus our Lord (Rom. 6:23)."

Underline the word wages.

Circle the word death.

Draw an arrow between the two words.

We were living under an edict of destruction too. While we won't fully shed our sin nature this side of heaven, Christ allows us to walk in increasing measures of freedom. Our hope shifts from a life of slavery, ending in death, to a life of hope, ending in freedom. If we've walked with Christ long at all, it's easy to forget this.

The Passover was established by God to remind His people that they were once slaves, set free by a loving God. *We need to remember too.*

To close this day's study, make a list of all Christ has set you free from. Then plan a way to commemorate His work in your life. It could be a walk, like mine, with the miles marking the years since your salvation. It could be a work of art you create, a conversation you've been meaning to have with someone who doesn't know Christ, or simply a journal entry recording your list above.

The principles of the Passover are beneficial for all of God's children. Remember what He has saved you from and declare it in whatever ways you feel inspired to do so.

GOOD NEWS/BAD NEWS

BIG IDEA: *The Passover is a portrait of the gospel.*

READ EXODUS 12:1–13

When I teach the Bible in my home or church, I've made a commitment to ensure that every learner can clearly articulate the gospel. That may feel elementary, but years of opening the Bible with others has taught me that the gospel is not always a no-brainer. In part, that's because the gospel is supernatural, and therefore difficult to put into words. But sometimes, we're just rusty, out of practice in articulating the Good News that has transformed us.

Write out a definition of the gospel below.

There's no need to use fancy, spiritual words to try to drum up a complicated definition.

The gospel, at its core, is the bad news that, left to our own devices, we all run in glad rebellion *away* from the law God has established for our good. Our rebellion has consequences, *deadly consequences.*

That's the cloud. Here is the silver lining. Jesus Christ willingly died to pay the price that our sin requires.

What gospel promise did Jesus make in John 5:24?

Thousands of years before Christ spoke these words, He declared the same beautiful truth through the Passover.

GOOD NEWS/BAD NEWS

When someone prefaces their statement with, "I've got good news and I've got bad news . . ." which statement do you prefer to hear first? Circle one.

Give me the good news.   **Tell me the bad stuff.**

I'm a rip-off-the-Band-Aid kind of girl myself. Hit me with the hard stuff first (and don't sugarcoat it).

In Exodus 12, the nation of Israel faced a high stakes good news/bad news scenario.

Record the bad news found in verse 12.

This isn't just bad news, it's the kind of news that makes your heart stop, your knees shake, and your palms sweat. All of the firstborns in the land would be wiped out in a single night. In my immediate circle that would include:

My husband

My oldest son

My dad

My father-in-law

My pastor

Several close friends

(Not to mention many of the cows and sheep currently grazing in the fields behind my house).

BOYS ONLY?

I've always heard that the 10th plague meant the death of all firstborn males. But I don't see that clearly by looking at this single text. This is why hermeneutics matter! This method of interpretation serves as a guardrail to help us navigate tough passages. Where did the idea that the 10th plague killed males only come from?

A BRIEF HEBREW LESSON

The Bible wasn't originally written in our language. The book of Exodus, like the rest of the Old Testament, was originally written in Hebrew.

I asked Rabbi Lane for help with the language in this passage. He explained,

> B'khor/First-born is a technical (and legal) term which was operative not only among the Israelites but was common throughout the ancient Near East and many places around the

world (and still applies in several societies today). It refers to the firstborn male who by the right of primogeniture inherits the larger—or largest, or entire—estate of the paterfamilias, the male head of the family (see Deut. 21:15–17). So, when Exodus 11:4–5 and 12:12, 29 speak of B'khor/First-born of human beings, these texts technically are referring to the first male offspring.[7]

A DRAMATIC REVERSAL

Scholars also point out that this plague could be a reversal of the Pharaoh's edict to kill all male babies recorded in Exodus 1:16, "When you serve as midwife to the Hebrew women and see them on the birthstool, if it is a son, you shall kill him, but if it is a daughter, she shall live."

List the firstborn males in your inner circle.

This bad news was very, very bad.

Record the good news found in verse 13.

While the people of Egypt suffered unthinkable tragedy, the Israelites who obeyed God's commands by observing the Passover were spared. The angel literally *passed over* their homes, leaving the Israelite fathers and grandfathers, husbands and sons, sheep and goats sleeping safely in their beds.

Record the specific instructions given to Moses and Aaron for the first Passover.

Instructions for the Passover lamb (vv. 3–6, 21)

Instructions for the doorposts (vv. 7, 22)

Instructions for eating (vv. 8–10)

Instructions for clothing/preparedness (v. 11)

Go back and circle any of these instructions that point to the gospel.

Can you imagine the faith required for God's people to follow these instructions? Remember how long they'd been enslaved. (Hint: you recorded the answer in Week One, Day 2).

It makes me wonder . . . how many nights had they prayed for freedom? How many generations had passed without relief? And now . . . deliverance was promised through circumstances that must have felt *unbelievable.*

If you'd heard these instructions, what questions or hesitations would you have?

Fortunately for them (and for us) the nation of Israel obeyed the commands of God. (See verse 28).

READ EXODUS 12:29–32

How was Pharaoh personally impacted by this tenth and final plague?

Death was required for God's people to walk in freedom. Pharaoh ignored nine previous plagues. He turned a deaf ear to all of Moses's and Aaron's pleading. But through the death of his own child, his heart was changed, and the Israelites were set free.

Write down Pharaoh's exact words recorded in verses 31–32.

"Up, go." This was the emancipation proclamation of the people of God. They were free to flee the land where they'd been enslaved and return to the land God had promised. With every step they took, they were declaring the gospel. They had been delivered from death to a life of freedom. If they'd known the words, they surely would have been humming *Amazing Grace* as they fled.

Wrap up today's study by reading John 5:1–18. What form of slavery did this man endure?

What words did Jesus say to him (v. 8)?

In other words, "Up, go!" Live free from your bondage in Jesus' name. Again we see the gospel on display. While both the first Passover and the miracles of Christ were actual events—recorded on the literal timeline of history—they are also telling the story of all mankind.

How does Romans 6:17 describe our condition before Christ?

Remember, I'm not a fan of sugarcoating. We're all crippled by our sin nature and enslaved as a result. It is the bad news of our true condition without Christ that makes the good news of the gospel so sweet.

THE PASSOVER LAMB

BIG IDEA: *The blood of the Passover Lamb covers our sin.*

READ 1 PETER 1:17–21

Spring is lambing season on the Davis farm.

Just about the time the frost stops covering the ground each morning and spring buds appear on the trees in our orchard, our momma lambs start birthing their babies. With bright white wool, tiny pink noses, and adorable little "baa" sounds, newborn lambs are about the sweetest, purest things I can imagine.

One year, during Lenten season, I stood at the fence and watched a flock of baby lambs playing in the grass. Suddenly, a terrible thought struck me. How would I feel if someone entered our pasture and murdered our sweet lambs? Unthinkable! Who would dare harm something so precious? So pure?

And yet, this is the picture of what happened to Christ. His heart was as pure as a newborn lamb's coat. His life was spotless, free from the marks of sin. And still, He was murdered for sins He did not commit, crucified for us.

It's both unthinkable and true.

Long before that terrible moment, when history was split in two by Christ's crucifixion, God declared His coming sacrifice to His people through the blood of the Passover lamb.

Use the prompts below to record the specific instructions given through Moses and recorded in Exodus 12:3–13.

What day are they to separate a lamb from the flock (v. 3)?

A lamb was to be sacrificed on behalf of every what (v. 3)? Circle the correct answer.

    Child   Person   Household   Male

How were small families instructed to observe this command (v. 4)?

The lamb was to be male *or* female *(circle one) and without* _____ *(v. 5). Underline that verse in your Bible. (Keep reading to see why.)*

How old was the lamb? What pen did it need to come from (v. 5)?

How many days did they keep the lamb (compare verses 3 and 6)?

What was Israel instructed to do on the fourteenth day (v. 6)?

For practical purposes, any ol' lamb would do. The Israelites were just going to kill the lambs anyway. Why not allow them to slaughter older sheep or those who were undesirable for future breeding? Because God was teaching His people a parable. By sacrificing the Passover lamb, God's people were telling a story pointing forward to Jesus, the spotless Lamb who was chosen as a sacrifice for our sins.

Use the chart below to compare the lamb required in Exodus 12 with Christ, our Passover Lamb.

EXODUS 12:5	1 PETER 1:19

Circle all similarities between these two "lambs."

Peter was referencing the first Passover as he wrote about Christ, the Lamb. *Read through the passage below from 1 Peter 1.*

Circle any language that references slavery or deliverance.

Underline anything that reminds you of the first Passover lamb.

Highlight any part of this passage that reminds you of the gospel.

> [17] And if you call on him as Father who judges impartially according to each one's deeds, conduct yourselves with fear throughout the time of your exile, [18] knowing that you were ransomed from the futile ways inherited from your forefathers, not with perishable things such as silver or gold, [19] but with the precious blood of Christ, like that of a lamb without blemish or spot. [20] He was foreknown before the foundation of the world but was made manifest in the last times for the sake of you [21] who through him are believers in God, who raised him from the dead and gave him glory, so that your faith and hope are in God.

Not only was the type of lamb telling a story about Christ on the first Passover, the specific instructions given to Israel about what to do with the lamb were prophetic.

Review Exodus 12:7–13.

Where were the Israelites to place the blood of their Passover lamb?

In addition to the doorposts, the lamb's blood was to be brushed onto the "lintel" of each home.

What is a lintel, exactly? It's the horizontal support that spans an opening in a structure (in this case, a door).

This is more than an ancient architecture lesson. And a lintel isn't just a pretty feature made for Pinterest pins. God was instructing His people to place the blood of the lamb on the *load bearing beams of their homes*. (Are you ready for this? It's about to get good!)

What was the sign to the angel to pass over the homes of God's people (v. 13)?

Write out the following passages:

Acts 20:28

Romans 5:9

Colossians 1:20

What covers our sin, allowing us to be spared from the wages of sin?

THE BLOOD OF CHRIST!

I am sorry for yelling at you there, but this makes me want to stand up on my chair and whoop. When it comes to our sin . . . *the blood of Christ bears the load.*

Jesus is the perfect, spotless lamb. Because of His blood, we are spared, death has passed us over, eternal life is ours instead.

Messianic Jewish Bible teacher Zola Levitt said it this way,

> Back to the meaning of Passover; it is surely the feast of salvation. On this day, because of the blood of the Lamb ("without blemish, a male . . ." Exodus 12:5) the Hebrew nation was delivered from bondage. Clearly, in both Testaments, the blood of the Lamb delivers from slavery—the Jew from Egypt, the Christian from sin.[8]

Take time to worship Christ for His sacrifice on your behalf today. Use Revelation 5:9–12 as your guide as you express your awe and gratitude to the perfect Lamb, slain for you.

BORN AGAIN

BIG IDEA: *The Passover tells the story of re-birth.*

READ JOHN 3:1–8

"Every time women get together, they cry and talk about childbirth."

This was the observation of the husband of one of my friends. He's right. Gather women who have experienced the miracle of childbirth together and sooner or later the conversation usually drifts in that direction. We will inevitably start comparing notes on the number of hours we spent in labor and the physical price we paid to bring our babies into the world. (I delivered my babies in 36 hours, 28 hours, 12 hours, and 7 hours, if you're wondering).

I had a doula help with the delivery of my second son. She'd witnessed the birth of hundreds of babies. As she shared some of their stories, she made a fascinating observation. She told me that she could ask a woman to record the birth story of her child hours after delivery. She'd been doing the work long enough that she had repeated the exercise with women years after they gave birth. Even then, most mothers are able to remember every detail of their baby's delivery. That's how clearly, and permanently, a woman remembers giving birth.

As I sat across the table from Rabbi Lane, I asked him what symbolism he saw in the first Passover. "It's a birth story," he replied simply. "Because ultimately what

Passover represents is the birth of a people, or at least the story about how the people came to be."[9]

Though it would be an overstatement to say that the Passover was meant to parallel childbirth, Rabbi Lane's words did help me see this story in new ways.

Let's look again at these passages and consider this analogy together.

Who doesn't love a good birth story? This one begins like all of ours did, with birth pains.

Record each of the ten plagues, found in the verses listed.

PLAGUE #1
Exodus 7:17–20

PLAGUE #2
Exodus 8:1–6

PLAGUE #3
Exodus 8:16–18

PLAGUE #4
Exodus 8:20–24

PLAGUE #5

Exodus 9:1–7

PLAGUE #6

Exodus 9:8–11

PLAGUE #7

Exodus 9:22–28

PLAGUE #8

Exodus 10:12–15

PLAGUE #9

Exodus 10:21–23

PLAGUE #10

Exodus 11:4–6

Much like early labor, the pain of the plagues ebbed and flowed. After each one, there was a period of relief.

Scripture doesn't reveal how long all of the plagues lasted, but the book of Exodus does give us this information for plagues 1, 9, and 10. Use the chart below to record this information.

THE PLAGUE	HOW LONG THE PLAGUE LASTED
Plague #1: Water turned to blood (Ex. 7:25)	
Plague #9: Deep darkness (Ex. 10:22)	
Plague #10: Death of the firstborn (Ex. 11:4)	

Does anything stand out to you about the variation in the length of these three plagues?

Do any patterns seem to point to birth imagery?

The plagues occurred as a progression of increasing intensity. The Egyptians started out by swatting away gnats and flies but were eventually covered in darkness and death. The plagues were never meant to go on forever. God planned a beginning, a middle, and an end to this terrible chapter in Egypt's history. Though certainly a demonstration of God's unmatched power, the plagues were so much more. These were the birth pains that would ultimately lead to the delivery of God's people.

Read Exodus 12:11. Record the Lord's instructions to His people.

Why did God ask the Israelites to eat the Passover meal in this way?

God's people knew there would be a Passover. They knew it was important and they knew about when it would come, *but not exactly.* Like new mommies and daddies who pack their hospital bag and leave it waiting by the back door, His people needed to be ready to move quickly once it was time.

After the plague of the firstborn, the Israelites followed God's command and fled Egypt.

READ EXODUS 14
Record the highlights of what happened after they fled.

God broke the water of the Red Sea to give His people safe passage through the "birth canal." This delivery was supernatural; the Israelites couldn't do it on their own. The people of God were dependent on Him every step of the way.

What circumstances has God used in your life to expose your dependence on Him?

As they stood on the banks of the Red Sea following their delivery, the Israelites partied. They sang (Ex. 15:1). They danced (v. 20). They even had a conga line (v. 20). Is it possible this was a birthday party?

Revisit John 3:1–8. Let's break it down.

What did Nicodemus say in verse 2?

Nicodemus was making a statement of faith, acknowledging both the existence of God and God's hand on Jesus' life. Yet, the gospel is so much more than just saying that there is a God or even that God sometimes works in the lives of others.

Jesus responds to Nicodemus with a deep truth. *Record His words below, found in verse 3.*

"Born again." It's a phrase we might throw around without a second thought. Yet we never see those words together in Scripture prior to this interaction between Jesus and Nicodemus. From a human perspective, this was a new idea!

No wonder Nicodemus took Jesus literally and wondered out loud how he could possibly experience physical birth again. (As a momma of children who are now nearly as tall as I am, I'm with Nicodemus on ruling that idea out!) How does Jesus address Nicodemus's reservations in verses 5–6?

Jesus shared the gospel with Nicodemus in beautifully simple terms. *Write down His words recorded in John 3:15.*

Let's keep reading. You might be able to fill in the blanks for the next verse without even looking.

"For _____ so _____ the _____, that he gave his only _____, that whoever _____ in _____ should not _____ but have _____ _____" (v. 16).

This most-often-quoted verse in the Bible is the gospel in its simplest, sweetest form. Jesus wasn't asking Nicodemus to journey back through his momma's birth canal (whew!). Instead, He was pointing out that because of his sin nature, Nicodemus's heart needed a re-birth.

The Israelites who celebrated the very first Passover had already been physically born. Nicodemus was right, they couldn't enter their mother's womb a second time.

This was a rebirth—a chance to live life anew, this time as the free children of God.

Once again, the events of the first Passover point forward toward gospel hope.

Close today's study by meditating on 1 Peter:1:3–9. *What hope do we have in Jesus as His born-again children?*

TWILIGHT

BIG IDEA: *When darkness surrounds us, God's Word helps us see the light.*

READ JOHN 1:4–5

There are times when I suffer from brokenness fatigue.

I look around at the brokenness . . .
. . . in my own heart and home . . .
. . . in the hearts and homes of the people I love . . .
. . . in the bodies of people I go to church with . . .
. . . in the lives of people who fill my social media feeds . . .
. . . in our culture . . .
. . . in our world . . .

And I feel weary in the very marrow of my bones.

The Bible is not a book filled with unicorns and rainbows that glosses over the devastating reality of life in a world broken by sin. Instead, we are reminded, "For we do not wrestle against flesh and blood, but against the rulers, against the authorities, against the cosmic powers over this present darkness, against the spiritual forces of evil in the heavenly places" (Eph. 6:12).

This present darkness has been present since the garden of Eden. It will remain with us until Christ's return. How do we cope with being children of light in a darkened world? How do we cling to our gospel hope when brokenness fatigue threatens to settle in?

Let's turn our attention toward the first Passover again and remember, there is a light that outshines the darkness.

READ EXODUS 12:6

What time of day were the Israelites instructed to kill the Passover lamb?

As the sun descended on their last day as slaves, the Israelites were instructed to kill the Passover lamb as an act of faith. Perhaps it felt like bad timing. Darkness is so rarely a comfort. More often it's a source of anxiety and doubt. And yet, even as darkness fell, hope was being sprinkled on the doorposts of God's beloved. Though their feelings must have protested, God's people were staking their claim on His promises.

Where do you see spiritual darkness most prevalently?

List the circumstances that are currently giving you brokenness fatigue.

It's so easy to focus on this present darkness and, as a result, to gravitate toward hopelessness. In moments of twilight . . . when darkness seems to be swallowing the light whole, God's Word helps us shift our focus away from the brokenness around us and onto the promises of God.

Let's revisit John 1:4–5.

> In him was life, and the life was the light of men. The light shines in the darkness, and the darkness has not overcome it.

Circle the word life *any time it appears in the text.*

Underline the word light *any time it appears in the text.*

Highlight the word darkness *any time it appears in the text.*

The apostle John wrote these words sometime between A.D. 70 and A.D. 100. As a member of Jesus' inner circle during His earthly ministry, John had witnessed Christ's arrest, crucifixion, and burial with his own eyes.

Record the event that John must have witnessed recorded in Mark 15:33.

John knew darkness. And yet he reminds us that the spiritual darkness that covers the earth—and the Prince of Darkness who seeks to destroy us—will never, ever overcome the Light. When we fear the darkness will overtake us, God's Word is the switch that turns our attention back to the Light of the World.

What do each of the following verses teach us about Jesus and light?

Matthew 4:16

John 8:12

1 John 1:5–9

Revelation 21:23

What do each of the following verses teach us about us and light?

Matthew 5:16

John 12:35–37

1 Peter 2:9

When the Lord gave Moses instructions for the Seven Feasts, the Passover topped the list.

READ LEVITICUS 23:4–8

In what month were the Israelites supposed to observe the Passover feast? On what day?

What time of day did the Passover feast start?

Each new year would bring new waves of darkness for God's people, as each new year does for us. Yet God established the Jewish calendar so that very early in the year, at twilight as darkness fell, God's people would remember their heritage.

They were slaves, set free. A people reborn. Spared from death by the blood of the Lamb. And called to live as children of the Light.

When brokenness fatigue settles into my bones . . . when the darkness feels oppressive . . . when I'm struck once again with brokenness fatigue . . . I need these reminders too.

Here are five Passover reminders for us to cling to as we wait for the Light to return. *Since repetition sears truth deeply past the superficial layers of our hearts, write these reminders out below each statement.*

1. I was once a slave to sin. Christ has set me free.

2. The blood of Christ covers my sin, allowing death to pass over me.

3. Through Christ, I am born again. I am a new creation.

4. Jesus is the Light of the World. Darkness will not overcome me.

5. As God's child, I am a bearer of light.

READ MATTHEW 26:17-25

For which religious feast did Jesus and the disciples gather to celebrate?

READ MATTHEW 26:26-29

What new instructions did Jesus give for how to remember the beautiful truths showcased at Passover?

Flip back to Leviticus 23:4–8. How long did the Passover last?

Within a few hours of this Passover feast, Christ would be arrested, tried, and crucified. In His divine timing, our Passover Lamb was killed on Passover, following the pattern He established way back in Leviticus 23.

How are we called to observe the Passover in these days? We live as children of the light and "proclaim the Lord's death until he comes" (1 Cor. 11:26).

Conclude today's study by writing Psalm 139:11–12 as a prayer, thanking God that His light always shines brighter than the darkness.

3 QUESTIONS FOR GROUP STUDY

1. What does this tell us about God?

2. What does this tell us about us?

3. How should we respond?

The Feast of Unleavened Bread

"Give us this day our daily bread" (Matt. 6:11). These are the words given to us by Jesus as He taught us to pray.

Perhaps, like me, you've always thought Jesus was training us to ask for His help with our *physical* needs. The Feast of Unleavened Bread teaches us to ask for so much more.

As pastor John Piper puts it, "Jesus did not come into the world mainly to give bread, but to be bread."[10]

Christ told us so Himself, "I am the bread of life; whoever comes to me shall not hunger, and whoever believes in me shall never thirst" (John 6:35).

And again . . . "I am the bread of life" (v. 48).

And again . . . "I am the living bread that came down from heaven. If anyone eats of this bread, he will live forever. And the bread that I will give for the life of the world is my flesh" (v. 51).

The Feast of Unleavened Bread begins the night after Passover. These two feasts are mentioned separately in Leviticus 23. Today, the feasts of Passover, Unleavened Bread, and Firstfruits are celebrated together as part of the Passover feast. While the Passover is meant to remind us of our deliverance from death, the Feast of Unleavened Bread reminds us that we still face the dangerous and permeating effect of sin.

That is why we must learn to pray for "daily bread," not meaning more toast or another warm baguette, but more of Jesus, our daily "Bread." May you turn to Him again this week and rest in the promise that He is willing and able to cleanse you of sin and transform you into something brand new.

THROW IT OUT

BIG IDEA: *God's Word reminds us to rid ourselves of the sin that once permeated our lives.*

READ 1 CORINTHIANS 5:6–8

In our newly married years, we lived in a tiny house surrounded by other tiny houses. One of our favorite neighbors was Sharon, a white-headed grandma who adopted us as her own. Over time, I've found my way around the kitchen and developed a deep passion for cooking; but back then, my recipe repertoire was limited to tacos and . . . well, tacos.

Sharon, on the other hand, had a culinary talent I greatly admired—bread baking! She kept a sourdough starter in her fridge, and each week, she'd pull out a lump, add a few additional ingredients, throw it into the oven and voila! Heaven. Many years later, my mouth still waters at the thought of Miss Sharon's bread.

The process of bread baking is a parable, used throughout Scripture to teach us about the permeating power of sin in our lives. We turn our attention toward the second feast, The Feast of Unleavened Bread, as a means to examine the sin that so easily works its way into our hearts and homes.

Before we zero in on our key passage, let's practice widening the lens to look for the bigger picture. *Answer the following questions about the book of 1 Corinthians.*

Who wrote 1 Corinthians (v. 1:1)?

Who did he write this letter to (v. 2)?

What do we know about the intended audience (v. 2)?

How would you describe the writer's tone toward his readers in verses 4–9?

According to verses 10–11, what prompted Paul to write this letter to his Corinthian brothers and sisters?

Paul loved the believers in Corinth. His letter opens with gratitude for this group of disciples as well as a strong reminder of their true identity in Christ. Yet, 1 Corinthians is not a warm and fuzzy letter. It is full of pastoral pleas for unity, faithfulness, and—as we'll see—sexual purity.

In 1 Corinthians 5:6–8, Paul gives an important analogy for sin that applies to all of our lives. Before we get there, let's pay attention to what is happening in the surrounding verses.

What specific sin was rumored to be occurring within the Corinthian church?

Well, this is awkward. A man *within the church* was sleeping with his father's wife.

Write out the command given in Leviticus 18:8.

This Corinthian pair was not the first to test the boundaries of holiness in this matter. Way back in Leviticus 18, as God was outlining the law for the liberated Israelites, there was a need to call out this specific practice as immoral.

If this was happening in your church, how do you think you'd respond?

According to verse 2, what heart attitude did the church have toward this man's sin?

We don't know if they were arrogant in their celebration of this immoral sexual relationship, perhaps thinking of themselves as "tolerant," or if, instead, they were arrogant in their assumption that they were not equally as capable of violating God's law. Either way, the Corinthian church responded to evidence of sin in their fellowship with pride instead of humility.

How did Paul ask them to respond to sin instead?

Within the context of dealing with sin within the church, Paul gives an analogy that applies to *all believers* in *every church.*

Reread 1 Corinthians 5:6–8. Circle in your Bible the words leaven *and* unleavened *every time they appear.*

Since we pick up our bread in a bag at the grocery store, the nuances of what Paul is teaching here can easily be lost on us. In bread baking, leaven is the substance used to make the bread rise by creating tiny air bubbles within the dough. We use pre-packaged yeast to accomplish the desired rise in modern bread baking practices, but the Corinthians were more likely to have relied on fermented dough, carried over from week to week, loaf to loaf, just like Miss Sharon's sourdough starter.

Once a leavening agent is introduced into dough, there's no extracting it. It works its way into every nook and cranny so that the entire loaf rises. Paul's reminder is that sin has the same effect. Tolerating even a "little bit" of sin will change the structure of our hearts, our homes, our churches, and our culture.

Match the following references with the correct statement about sin.

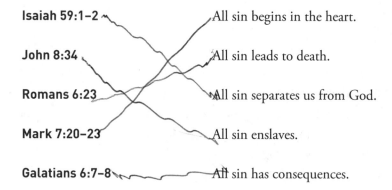

Isaiah 59:1–2   All sin begins in the heart.

John 8:34   All sin leads to death.

Romans 6:23   All sin separates us from God.

Mark 7:20–23   All sin enslaves.

Galatians 6:7–8   All sin has consequences.

Go back to the list on the right and circle the word "all" every time it appears. Now go back and underline the word "all" every time it appears. One more time, with feeling, draw an arrow pointing to the word "all" every time it appears.

I know that was redundant, but we need this truth pounded into our sinful and broken hearts: *all sin matters, because all sin is offensive to our holy God.*

Sin almost never starts with something as flagrant as sleeping with our step-parent. Most often, it is a series of compromises, a slow slide away from holiness and toward gratifying our sinful flesh.

Can you think of a time when a "little" bit of sin worked its way into your life through a seemingly minor compromise? What was the result? Write about this below.

We see in James 1:14–15 that the progression from temptation to embracing sin occurs in three steps. *Read this passage and fill in the blanks for the steps below.*

STEP 1: "But each person is tempted when he is lured and enticed by his own _desire_ " (v. 14).

STEP 2: "Then desire when it has conceived gives birth to _sin_ " (v. 15).

STEP 3: "And sin when it is fully grown brings forth _death_ " (v. 15).

The road between our desires and our destruction is alarmingly short, a single step called sin. There's no such thing as just a little leaven in a loaf of bread and there's no such thing as a little sin in our own lives.

Because of this deadly progression, what does Paul remind believers to do with the old leaven (sin) in our lives? (1 Cor. 5:7).

To conclude today's study, write out a prayer to the Lord. Invite Jesus to expose any sin that has worked its way into your life and express your desire to throw out the "old leaven" of sin once again.

NEW LUMPS

BIG IDEA: *The gospel doesn't simply change us to a less sinful version of ourselves, the gospel transforms us into a new creation.*

READ 2 CORINTHIANS 5:17–21

It's been a long time since I was a newlywed who didn't know the difference between a whisk and a spatula. My husband will gratefully inform you he eats far fewer tacos these days as I've become a bread baker myself.

Learning to bake bread requires a commitment to the process of trial and error. Bread is notoriously finicky and ingredients must be measured meticulously to create the perfect crumb and rise. Unlike other forms of cooking, you can't just add a little more of this or take out a little bit of that. Once a batch goes south, you might as well toss it into the trash and start again.

Committing to rid our lives of sin can feel more frustrating than the process of learning to bake bread. No matter how badly we want to, we cannot shed the sin nature that comes with being human. We can commit to rid our lives of "old leaven" in one breath, and sin in the next. This can lead to a cycle of discouragement that makes us fear that God will toss us out in frustration.

In those moments, we need reminders of how the gospel has transformed us, rhythms of remembrance that point us toward Christ's work in us.

Let's revisit Paul's words from 1 Corinthians 5:6–8. What kind of "lump" (or "batch," NIV) does he encourage the Corinthian believers to be?

Notice Paul doesn't call us to become a better lump, a purer version of our previous selves. Instead, he reminds us we are a "new lump" (v. 7), something altogether different than we were before.

When you think of your life before and after Christ, what evidence do you see that you've been made new?

JESUS, (UNLEAVENED) BREAD OF LIFE

READ JOHN 6:32–48

Write down any bread references you find.

What do each of the following verses teach us about Jesus?

Hebrews 4:15

2 Corinthians 5:21

1 Peter 2:22

Since leaven is used throughout Scripture as a symbol for sin, unleavened bread represents life without sin. Jesus lived a life in the flesh and yet never sinned. He is pure, utterly free of the contamination of leaven/sin in His life. *Just as the spotless Passover lamb is a picture for Christ's purity, the unleavened bread God asked His people to eat during the Feast of Unleavened Bread is a picture of His sinlessness.* Jesus, the Bread of Life, is untainted by the leaven of sin.

Christ's identity changes our identity. *Rewrite these verses using "I am" statements.*

2 Corinthians 5:17

I am . . .

Galatians 2:20

I am . . .

Romans 6:1–4

I am . . .

Fill in the blanks to complete Paul's reminder from 1 Corinthians 5:7.

"Cleanse out the old leaven that you may be a new lump, _____ _____ _____
_____ _____. For Christ, our Passover lamb, has been sacrificed."

What do you think Paul meant when he said "you really are unleavened"?

There are a lot of days I don't feel like a "new creation." Because I've not yet reached the sinless perfection Christ modeled and called me to, I tend toward discouragement. While I am confident in my *salvation* and Christ's saving work on the cross, I grow weary in my *sanctification*, the Spirit-filled process of becoming like Him. Do you?

What discourages you about Christ's sanctifying work in your own life? How about in the lives of others?

The Corinthians must have been weary too because Paul needed to remind them of their identity in Christ. He wrote, "you really are unleavened." Translation, you really are transformed by Christ's power. No, really. It's true.

Go back to the I am statements you just wrote. Next to each one write "I really am."

I understand these statements may not *feel* true. But if you've given your life to Christ, this is who He declares you to be. Though the process is hard to see at times, God is at work to purify you and make you more like Him. No, really. It's true.

Paul called the Corinthian believers to rid their lives of the leaven of sin. While we cannot turn from sin apart from Christ, Paul's words remind us that sanctification does involve some action on our part. Read his words once again:

Cleanse out the old leaven that you may be a new lump, as you really are unleavened. For Christ, our Passover lamb, has been sacrificed (1 Cor. 5:7).

Underline the last sentence in this passage.

If cleansing our lives is the *what*, Christ's sacrifice is the *how*. We can become "new lumps," free from the destructive power of sin in our lives because Christ lived a sinless life and then died as our Passover Lamb.

Focusing on *your* sin and *your* powerlessness over sin can never make you new. But shift your gaze to Jesus, your sinless Savior, and see that He is more than able to transform you completely, *to make you brand new.*

Wrap up today's study by reading Revelation 4. Circle the word holy *any time it appears in the text. Instead of focusing on your sin today, focus on the unmatched holiness of your God.*

RHYTHMS OF CONFESSION

BIG IDEA: *We confess. Christ cleanses.*

READ PSALM 51

Lucille's sourdough starter is older than the Wright brothers' airplane. Sitting in her fridge is a sourdough starter that Lucille's family has traced all the way back to 1889. Lucille's sourdough starter is a survivor. It has lived through the Great Depression, two world wars, and the War on Terror. It has lived in an American refrigerator under the leadership of twenty-four United States presidents. Lucille got the starter from her momma. Her momma got it from a student at the University of Wyoming. That student traced the origin of the starter all the way back to 1889, to a Wyoming sheepherder's wagon. What does Lucille do with her ancient dough? Mostly, she makes killer pancakes.[11]

Was I buttering you up with all of that pancake talk? Maybe. Because today we're still talking about sin, specifically, our responsibility when it comes to cleansing the sin from our lives. While sin makes us uncomfortable, God's clear desire is to expose sin so that we might live free.

Don't you love how the Bible uses what we know in the flesh to help us understand what we struggle to understand in the spirit? We understand Lucille's sourdough. In the back of a wagon, leaven transformed flour to dough and there was no going back. There's no way to extract the leaven and start over with pure flour again.

We also understand that the dough got passed from generation to generation. The Bible helps us transfer our knowledge of the world around us to what we need to know about our true spiritual condition. Way back in the garden of Eden pure humanity was tainted by sin. There's no going back. Just like Lucille's dough, sin and its consequences get passed from generation to generation.

As followers of Christ, who desire to live holy and upright lives, we must watch for, and be willing to rid ourselves of, all sin. But how? Our sin nature is superglued to us. We cannot separate ourselves from it.

Read Paul's words found in Romans 7:15–20. Rewrite them in your own words below.

Surely you also feel the tension of this spiritual tug of war.

What is one area of your life where you repeatedly do what you do not want to do?

What is one area of your life where you do not do something you desperately want to do?

READ HEBREWS 12:1

Draw a picture of how this verse describes sin.

READ EXODUS 34:6–7

What do we learn about God from these verses?

What do we learn about sin from these verses?

This is the devastating reality of generational sin. The consequences of sin can be passed, like a bad gene code, from generation to generation.

Maybe your mom struggled with bitterness, and now you do too. Maybe your grandfather was an addict, and so are your cousins. Maybe you see your ugly sin patterns starting to repeat in the lives of your children.

Because we share a sin nature inherited from Adam and Eve, we're all sinners. Sometimes that leads to patterns of sin, passed down the line like Lucille's lump of dough.

Read and record the Lord's instructions for the Feast of Unleavened Bread found in Leviticus 23:6–8.

Based on what you know about the purpose of the feasts, and the theme of leaven/ sin throughout the Bible, why do you think God commanded His people to observe this annual feast?

Maybe when you read Paul's words from 2 Corinthians 5:7, you respond with eagerness, ready to rid your life of the leaven of sin. But there's a problem: you can't—at least not on your own. So how *do* sinners go to war against sin? *Write out the hope-filled answer found in 1 John 1:9.*

When it comes to sin, what's our responsibility?

When it comes to sin, what's Christ's responsibility?

We confess. Christ cleanses. We adopt a zero tolerance policy toward sin in our own lives, acknowledging that even a little sin will eventually work its way into the nooks and crannies of our hearts, and we repent and believe the gospel to cleanse us and make us new.

What two words are used to describe God in this passage?

Because God is just, He will deal with your sin. Because He is faithful, He will stick with you in your sanctification, carefully cleansing you of everything that separates you from Him.

While 1 John 1:9 asks us to confess our sin to God, the book of James encourages us to keep confessing.

According to James 5:16, who are we to confess our sins to?

Since Christ's forgiveness is sufficient to cover our sins, why does God's Word teach us to confess to each other?

Nothing causes spiritual amnesia quite like sin does. Sin warps our hearts and minds, causing us to forget the promises and plans of God. When that happens, we need the encouragement, prayers, and support of other Christ followers. When you confess your sin to another Christian, you are opening up a pipeline of blessing by which you can be both held accountable for your sin and reminded of the gospel hope that is yours in Jesus. You cannot cleanse your own life of sin. Your friends can't do it for you. But you can look each other in the eyes, humbly confess your need for Jesus, and then remind each other of this bedrock truth.

> If we confess our sins, he is faithful and just to forgive us our sins and to cleanse us from all unrighteousness. (1 John 1:9)

To conclude today's study, read through Psalm 51. This psalm was written by King David after he faced his own sin. Use his prayer as a guide for how to pray about your sin.

HURRY!

BIG IDEA: *The need to run from sin, and toward Jesus, is urgent.*

READ EXODUS 12:15–20

He was handsome. She was rich. He was hard-to-get. She was filled with desire. And . . . no one was watching. No one would know.

Don't worry. You didn't accidentally trade in your Bible study for a steamy romance novel. This story actually comes straight from Scripture. (Though it is a little on the steamy side).

Read the account of Joseph and Potiphar's wife found in Genesis 39. Write down anything that stands out to you related to the topic of sin.

Joseph didn't flirt with sin. He didn't dabble in it. He didn't inch ever closer to sin's flame, hoping he wouldn't get burned.

According to verse 12, how did Joseph respond to temptation?

According to verse 11, what motivated his quick response?

Psalm 51:4 teaches us to add one more item to our list of things that are true about *all* sin. Even when our sin hurts others, according to this verse, who do we ultimately sin against?

Joseph wasn't worried about offending his boss. He wasn't motivated by appeasing Potiphar's wife. His primary concern wasn't what others would think of his behavior.

Joseph feared the Lord. He was motivated to flee from sin by his desire to honor a holy God.

The Feast of Unleavened Bread not only reminds us of the pervasive power of sin in our lives, it teaches us to turn from sin quickly, and to turn to Jesus before the leaven of sin works its way deep into our lives.

Revisit the account of the first Feast of Unleavened Bread recorded in Exodus 12:15–20. Remember what was happening in this moment. Fill in the blanks below.

God's people were enslaved in _____ (country).

They had prayed for and received a deliverer whose name was _____.

God sent _____ plagues on the nation of Egypt. God warned
His people through Moses that the tenth and final plague would be the

_____.

Before the final plague fell upon Egypt, God gave instructions on both the
Passover and the Feast of Unleavened Bread. *Write down the specific instructions
recorded in Exodus 12:15–20.*

READ EXODUS 12:33–34

What detail do we get about the bread of the Israelites from these verses?

Following the Exodus, the Israelites finished their first leg of what would become
a very long journey. Verse 37 tells us they journeyed from Ramses (a.k.a. Egypt,
Genesis 47:11) to their first campsite, Succoth.

What did they do once they set up camp (v. 39)?

Following the Exodus, the Lord again reminded His people about the Passover and
the Feast of Unleavened Bread, and commanded that these celebrations become
more than one-time events.

Write down the specific instructions given to God's people.

What consequences did God promise for those who did not obey? (Ex. 12:15, 19)

This is clearly about more than the type of bread the Israelites ate. The removal of leaven in their homes and lives was symbolic of their commitment to flee from sin and live under the commandments of God. An unwillingness to follow the simple and relatively painless command to eat unleavened bread was evidence of an unwillingness to obey God in larger matters; thus, those who refused were cut off from God's people by their disobedience.

Adding yeast or leaven to a loaf of bread is a long process. It takes time for bread to rise. Unleavened bread, on the other hand, symbolizes a quickness to get out of sin. Run! Flee! There's no time to prepare, to clean yourself up—the need to turn from sin is urgent.

For each of the following passages, circle the verb (or noun) that relates to sin.

No temptation has overtaken you that is not common to man. God is faithful, and he will not let you be tempted beyond your ability, but with the temptation he will also provide the way of escape, that you may be able to endure it. (1 Cor. 10:13)

Submit yourselves therefore to God. Resist the devil, and he will flee from you. (James 4:7)

**Repent therefore, and turn back, that your sins may be blotted out.
(Acts 3:19)**

Escape.
Resist.
Repent.
Turn back.

These verbs communicate urgency. Rather than allowing the debt of sin to pile up in our lives, we respond quickly and eagerly when God calls us to repentance through His Spirit. Understanding the corrosive and pervasive power of sin means we don't let sin sit in the "dough," convinced that it won't spread.

God convicts. We repent.
God convicts. We repent.
God convicts. We repent.

And when. . .

We repent. Christ forgives.
We repent. Christ forgives.
We repent. Christ forgives.

God is graciously inviting us into a new rhythm in which sin doesn't have the final say, and we are free to live as new lumps, cleansed by His resurrection power.

Dwell here for awhile. As long as it takes. **As you've studied the Feast of Unleavened Bread this week, has the Lord brought to mind an area of sin that needs to be cleansed? Is there sin in your life you need to quickly get out of?**

Are you waiting for the "yeast" to rise, thinking there will be a better, easier time to choose holiness? There isn't. There is urgency. No time to waste.

First, confess your sin to Him. Right now. Hurry!

Then, confess your sin to another Christian, asking them to pray for you to run away from your sin and rest in gospel hope.

THE CUP AND THE CRACKER

BIG IDEA: *When we take the Lord's Supper, we celebrate the hope found in the gospel.*

READ MATTHEW 26:17–29

Mind if I invite you into the most tender moment of my week?

C'mon. Have a seat with me in church. I sit with my husband and a group of close-knit friends. Each week we pack the pews, shoulder to shoulder, side by side. Usually one (or all) of us is holding a baby who is sick or fussy. We take turns passing their chubby bodies between us. We give hugs, we sing songs, and then we sit—and we remember.

I go to a communion-every-Sunday kind of church. My husband always grabs the tray of crackers and juice first. He holds it patiently, serving me communion, before taking it for himself. Somewhere along the line, the other husbands in our friend group started doing the same. All around me every Sunday there are husbands quietly and patiently serving their wives the bread and the cup.

After we eat and drink, we bow our heads. There are often tears. Sometimes someone has to make a Kleenex run.

I don't know what my friends and husband are praying for. I've never asked. But I know my communion prayers are almost always a version of "I'm sorry" and "thank you." Communion presses pause on the harried pace of my life. For a moment, I am free to look inside at the true condition of my heart. I am often overwhelmed by both my need for Jesus and His staggering grace.

Write about your own experience with communion.

How often do you take communion?

What does it symbolize to you?

What kinds of prayers do you pray as you take communion?

Jesus invites us into the Feast of Unleavened bread to reflect, repent, and worship. To better understand the significance of this feast, let's look at the Jewish calendar.

- Both the Passover and the Feast of Unleavened Bread occur in the Jewish month of Nisan (March).
- Preparations for the Passover begin on the fourteenth day of the month.

- The Feast of Unleavened Bread lasts seven days, beginning on the fifteenth day of the month.

N I S A N

1	2	3	4	5	6	7
8	9	10	11	12	13	14 Passover
15	16	17	18	19	20	21
		← Feast of Unleavened Bread →				
22	23	24	25	26	27	28
29	30					

According to Matthew 26:17, what day on the Jewish calendar were Jesus and His disciples gathered?

In line with Jewish tradition, Jesus and His disciples ate the Passover meal at sundown on Thursday evening, now Nisan (March) 15th.

Jesus was crucified the following afternoon. Because Jewish days go from sundown to sundown, Jesus was killed on Nisan (March) 15th, the same day He observed the Passover and the Feast of Unleavened Bread, then instituted the Lord's Supper with His disciples.

If navigating through centuries-old Jewish calendaring makes your head hurt, I understand. But the timing of the first Lord's Supper matters. Even as Jesus gathered with His friends . . . even as He reclined at the table . . . even as He passed the cup . . . He knew. He knew that *on that very day*, He would die a horrific death. He was fully aware that the next time the sun set, His body would be entombed in total darkness.

It was against that backdrop that He gave us the gift of the Lord's Supper. *Record His exact words written in Matthew 26:26–28.*

Jesus crammed so much into these few sentences.

- He prophesied His coming death (v. 28).
- He revealed the new covenant, secured by His blood (v. 28).
- He invited "many"—not just the twelve, not just Jews by birth, but many— to experience the forgiveness of sins (v. 29).
- He gave a glimpse of the coming hope that is ours in Him (v. 29).

These are life-changing, heart-satisfying, earth-shaking truths. And yet, Jesus is familiar with our chronic spiritual amnesia. In response, He gifts us a rhythm of remembrance of all He has done for us.

Because they were observing the Feast of Unleavened Bread, what kind of bread must Jesus and His disciples have eaten?

It wasn't just any bread He was breaking with His disciples. It was unleavened bread, symbolic of the sinless life He surrendered for us. Way back in Leviticus 23, when the Seven Feasts were written into the Israelite calendar, Jesus was telling a story, a gospel story of His coming sacrifice.

According to Matthew 27:46, what time did Jesus die?

This represents the ninth hour after dawn or 3 p.m.

According to Matthew 27:57–60, what time of day did Joseph bury Jesus' body?

Keeping in mind that the Jewish days begin at sundown, we can see that these events followed the pattern of the Seven Feasts with Passover beginning on the fourteenth day of the first month, and the Feast of Unleavened Bread the following day.

Christ was crucified on Passover and buried on the Feast of Unleavened Bread.

The tiny cracker we eat during communion tells the same story as the feasts: that Christ's sinless body was broken for us, His untainted blood was spilled on our behalf.

In Luke's account of this event, we get a phrase that jumps out at me. *Record Jesus' words from Luke 22:20.*

Circle the word this.

It's possible Jesus meant we were to remember the cross every time we ate bread and wine. But I don't think so. I think He was inviting us to a more frequent rhythm of remembrance.

I think it's every time we eat . . .

Every time we gather . . .

Every time we face a dark night of the soul like the disciples were about to . . .

We remember the cross, the price paid to ransom us. And we whisper as often as possible, "I'm sorry" and "thank you."

This is why we take communion. We are forcing our hearts to remember Christ's sacrifice on our behalf (the Feast of Passover) and taking the opportunity to evaluate the sin we need to run from (the Feast of Unleavened Bread).

To conclude this week's lesson, observe communion. Let the cracker and the juice remind you anew, "'This is my body, which is given for you. Do this in remembrance of me.' And likewise the cup after they had eaten, saying, 'This cup that is poured out for you is the new covenant in my blood.'" (Luke 22:19–20).

3 QUESTIONS FOR GROUP STUDY

1. What does this tell us about God?

2. What does this tell us about us?

3. How should we respond?

The Feast of Firstfruits

You're likely familiar with the story of Esther, the lowly orphan turned queen whose bold request saved the Jewish people from annihilation. You may not have realized that many of the events of the book of Esther occurred during the first three feasts.

The date Esther risked her life to petition King Ahasuerus fell on the Feast of Firstfruits (Est. 3:7–15, 5:1). As we will see in this week's study, this was a feast for the Promised Land, an opportunity for God's people to worship Him by giving Him back a portion of the abundant crops that were theirs in the land of milk and honey. Esther lived at a time when God's people had been captured and dragged away from their promised land. She had no sheep or grain of her own to dedicate to the Lord.

But this feast is about so much more.

This is a feast that celebrates that God gives us His very best: Himself. In return, as an act of worship, we give Him our very best.

Esther couldn't give the Lord the sheaves of grain and spotless lamb required in Leviticus 23. But she could give God her best. She did so by laying down her life to plead for mercy from a ruthless pagan king. Because she dedicated her "first fruits" to the Lord, Esther played a significant part in God's redemptive plan.

Esther's story is like the opening act before the best band ever. Something big happened during this feast a few hundred years later. Earth-shaking, history-splitting, death-reversing big.

As you study the Feast of Firstfruits, may you peek into the empty tomb with fresh awe, and respond in worship to the One who is worthy of our very best.

GARDENS AND THE GOSPEL

THE BIG IDEA: *Creation is constantly teaching us the gospel.*

READ LEVITICUS 23:9–14

The Bible is, among many other things, a farmer's almanac, filled with agrarian language. Many dots have been connected between God's Word and my own understanding of it when my hands are in the dirt. This is especially true of the Feast of Firstfruits.

Our farm works like an ever-expanding Sunday school classroom, filled with fruit-bearing plants. There's the orchard with apple and peach trees, the elderberry and blackberry patches, and the garden that started as patio tomatoes and has expanded throughout the years to cover more than an acre of ground. I've got an up close and personal view of the crop cycle, marking the seasons by the condition of my beloved plants.

Maybe you kill every plant that comes within a ten-mile radius. Perhaps you've never tasted a tomato you grew yourself or picked an apple from your very own tree. No shame, sista. A green thumb isn't required to love and learn from the Word of God.

But to understand this feast, we do need to understand at least one simple gardening principle—*the first fruit on the vine is worthy of celebrating.*

Draw a picture, or write the words that come to mind for each of the following seasons.

Fall   Summer

Winter   Spring

No offense to a day at the beach or pumpkin spice lattes, but we'll focus on winter and spring this week.

The words I'd used to describe winter include:

DARK

COLD   BLEAK

BARREN

Winter is the season in which the earth goes dormant. This part of the plant cycle is actually essential. Dropping their leaves and letting go of the demands of producing fruit allows plants to survive the colder temperatures and shorter daylight hours of winter. Plants must rest in order to continue to live out their God-given design year after year. *Friends, that will preach.*

Remind yourself what command God gave His people before He handed down the Seven Feasts (Hint: the answer is found in Lev. 23:3). *Write the command below:*

Creation has Sabbath built into its natural rhythms. Plants and animals know instinctively to operate within rhythms of rest. But the value of Sabbath isn't the only lesson our plants are teaching. Every bush, tree, and flower is proclaiming God's redemptive plan.

Read Romans 1:19. According to this verse, how can we grasp the invisible attributes of God?

Creation is constantly teaching us in parables. *What connections do each of the following passages make between creation and God's character?*

Lamentations 3:22–23

Isaiah 40:26

Job 37:21–23

Matthew 27:59–60 records what happened to Christ's body following His crucifixion: "And Joseph took the body and wrapped it in a clean linen shroud and laid it in his own new tomb, which he had cut in the rock. And he rolled a great stone to the entrance of the tomb and went away."

In each column of the chart below, write down any words that describe the two scenarios. Draw lines connecting any similarities.

In winter, plants...	The atmosphere in the tomb where Jesus was buried must have been...

Each winter, as creation goes dormant, it is telling the story of Christ's burial. Winter never lasts forever. Spring is an annual reminder that Christ did not stay buried, bursting onto the scene as a celebration of new life.

Birds hatch their babies.

Flowers push determinedly up through the ground with green leaves and colorful buds.

Fruit begins to form anew on trees, vines, and bushes.

The "firstfruits" of creation join together to declare this amazing truth . . .

> He is not here, for he has risen, as he said. Come, see the place where he lay. (Matt. 28:6)

Way back in Leviticus 23 . . .
Before we ever see the name of Jesus in Scripture . . .
Before the word "gospel" had ever been spoken . . .
Before the death, burial, and resurrection of our Savior . . .

God was teaching His people His redemptive plan by asking them to observe the Feast of Firstfruits.

This feast was not about giving God grain. God was showcasing the sacrificial system that would be fulfilled through Christ and turning Israel's attention to the annual appearance of new life all around them.

That's the abbreviated version. As we dig in during the days ahead, I pray you are delighted and encouraged by the depth of this feast.

To conclude this day's study, spend time in nature. What invisible attributes of God are obvious to you through creation? Write them down in the space below.

"COME AND SEE!"

BIG IDEA: *Jesus died on Passover, rested on the Sabbath, and rose on the Feast of Firstfruits.*

READ MATTHEW 28:1–15

One Easter I collapsed onto the couch after a full day of ham roasting, mashed potato making and eating, Easter egg hiding and hunting, and the level of exertion required to get four boys ready for church. As I surveyed the post-holiday state of my home, I looked around and saw brightly colored Easter eggs everywhere, cracked open and empty—and I couldn't help but smile.

I'm fond of saying that all truth is God's Truth. These plastic Easter eggs were telling a story, the story of Christ's empty tomb.

The empty tomb matters because it is proof that Jesus is alive. When God commanded this third feast, He was foretelling His own resurrection, sending shockwaves of hope throughout all of history.

The feasts are sequential.

When were God's people instructed to celebrate Passover (Lev. 23:5)?

When were God's people instructed to celebrate the Feast of Unleavened Bread? (Lev. 23:6)

Let's look carefully at the instructions for the third feast.

When did this feast take place? (Lev. 23:11)

The Jewish week begins on Sunday. *According to Leviticus 23:3, what day of the week was the Sabbath?*

Day 1 - Sunday

Day 2 - Monday

Day 3 - Tuesday

Day 4 - Wednesday

Day 5 - Thursday

Day 6 - Friday

Meaning the 7th day, the Sabbath day, was what day of the week?_____

Hold on tightly to that nugget. It matters. To see why, let's do a little more calendar work. Use the verses listed below to record the events for each day of Holy Week. Since it was a very full week and I don't want your hand to cramp, I've filled in some for you.

Sunday

Mark 11:1–10

What additional events are recorded in this passage?

• Jesus' triumphal entry into Jerusalem.

Monday

Mark 11:12–19

List the events recorded in these verses.

Tuesday

Mark 11:20–33

After a run-in with the religious leaders, Jesus moved on to teach the people in a series of parables. The list of the parables Jesus taught on this day includes the following:

• The two sons (Matt. 21:28–32)
• The tenants (Matt. 21:33–44)
• The marriage feast (Matt. 22:1–14)
• The fig tree (Matt. 24:32–35)

- The thief and the master (Matt. 24:36–44)
- The faithful vs. wicked servant (Matt. 24:45–51)
- The ten virgins (Matt. 25:1–13)
- The talents (Matt. 25:14–30)
- The sheep and the goats (Matt. 25:31–46)

Wednesday

Mark 14:1–11

- Religious leaders plotted to kill and arrest Jesus.
- Jesus was anointed with expensive oil by a woman at Bethany.
- Judas agreed to betray Jesus.

Thursday

List the events recorded in these passages.
Mark 14:12–25

Mark 14:32–50

Which brings us to Friday. The best/worst day ever when our Savior was brutally murdered for us.

Friday

- Jesus endured six trials in short order (John 18:12–27; Luke 22:66–71; 23:1–25).
- He was then publicly humiliated and forced to take a death march (Matt. 27; Mark 15; Luke 23; John 19).

- Jesus was crucified (Mark 15:25).
- Several hours later, Jesus died on the cross while His mother and followers watched (Mark 15:33–41).
- Joseph of Arimathea petitioned the court for Jesus' body, prepared it for burial and put it in the tomb (Mark 15:42–46).

Saturday

Jesus remained in the tomb.

What day of the week is the Jewish Sabbath?

Here's a question: Why didn't Jesus rise the day after He was killed? He certainly could have. He had the power to rise at any moment of His choosing.

Christ certainly had the right to rise on the Sabbath day. He informed the Pharisees that He was free to do good on the Sabbath, as were they (Matt. 12:12); but during Holy Week, the most important sequence of events ever, Jesus' body rested in the tomb on the Sabbath. Scripture doesn't state that Jesus didn't rise on the Sabbath in order to honor it, but in light of all we've learned about God's command to Sabbath, we can read about the resurrection timeline with fresh insight and interest. Is it possible that Jesus honored the Sabbath, established way back in Leviticus, and did no work on this day, not even the redemptive work of rising from the dead?

Sunday

The remarkable events of Resurrection Sunday are recorded in all four gospels: Matthew 28, Mark 16, Luke 24, and John 20.

Fill in the events left blank in the chart on the following page. You will see they are marked by white squares.

THE RESURRECTION IN ALL FOUR GOSPELS

	MATTHEW 28	MARK 16	LUKE 24	JOHN 20
What time was it?	Toward the dawn of the first day of the week	Very early on the first day of the week, when the sun had risen	On the first day of the week, at early dawn	(John 20:1)
Who went to the tomb?	Mary Magdalene & the other Mary	(Mark 16:1)	The women	Mary Magdalene

	MATTHEW 28	MARK 16	LUKE 24	JOHN 20
What happened?	(Matt. 28:2–20)	Women brought spices Angel speaks to the women The women fled tomb, but said nothing	The women take spices to tomb Two angels appear An angel speaks to the women Told the disciples what they found	Mary Magdalene ran to get Simon Peter Simon Peter and the other disciple went to the tomb The disciples left Jesus appeared to Mary
What did Jesus say?	(Matt. 28:9–10)			(John 20:15–17)

Though the four gospels were written years after Christ's birth by four different men, the facts are crystal clear.

- Jesus was crucified on Friday/Passover.
- He laid in the tomb on Saturday/Sabbath.
- And He rose from the dead on Sunday.

Circle back to Leviticus 23:11. What day was the Feast of Firstfruits?

God's Word is masterfully ordered! In Leviticus 23, God outlined His calendar of redemption for the nation of Israel, and here in the Gospels, Jesus observed the first three feasts as He was crucified, buried, and raised.

End today's lesson by reflecting on Ephesians 2:1–10. How does this passage make the pattern of death, burial, and resurrection personal in our own lives?

O GLORIOUS DAY!

BIG IDEA: *We are the second fruits of creation. One day soon, we will rise with Jesus.*

READ 1 CORINTHIANS 15:22–23

After a long, barren winter, the firstfruits of spring are a welcome miracle, but if there were no second fruits, the miracle would be short-lived. I don't just need one tomato; I need enough to make salsa. I don't want a single flower; I want bouquets and bouquets of colorful blooms. I can't bake an apple pie with one apple; I need a whole tree full of fruit.

Let's head back to 1 Corinthians. Think back to Week 3.

Who did Paul write this letter to?

What did he encourage Christians to rid their lives of?

Paul reminded the Corinthian believers that they had been made new through Christ, empowering them to turn from sin and live as "new lumps."

But how? That's the question I tend to ask when I think of the Bible's encouragement to live in my identity as a "new creation." Perhaps the Corinthians wondered the same, for Paul dedicated the words in the middle of this letter to practicalities like lawsuits among believers (6:1–8), principles for marriage (7:1–16), food practices (8:1–13), and spiritual gifts within the church (12:1–31).

When we get to chapter 15, the tone of Paul's letter changes. He's not writing about do's and don'ts anymore. He zeros in on what matters most: our gospel hope in Christ.

According to verses 3–4, what does Paul say is of first importance?

By connecting Christ's resurrection to the Feast of Firstfruits, Paul helps us see that the gospel is more than ancient history, *it is our future hope.*

READ 1 CORINTHIANS 15:20-28

Circle the word firstfruits *every time it appears.*

Underline the words raised *and* resurrection *every time they appear.*

Highlight the word Christ *every time it appears.*

What do you think it means that Christ is the "firstfruits of those who have fallen asleep" (v. 20)?

Let's think of the history of mankind like the seasons of the year for a moment.

In Genesis God created our world. It was a time of maximum fruitfulness much like summer, when the days are long and plants most productive.

Summer is followed by fall, in this case the fall of man as a result of Adam's and Eve's sin in the garden. The good gifts of God began to wither on the vine.

Fall is followed by winter. Since the garden, humanity has endured a spiritual winter. Sin stunts our growth. Death surrounds us. The days are dark.

But look to Christ! His resurrection is like the bud on a barren vine. There it is! Spring! New life! New hope! A sure sign that the long winter of sin and death is coming to an end.

Christ's life is the first evidence that death has been conquered. And where there is firstfruit, there will certainly be seconds.

Let's revisit 1 Corinthians 15:22–24. What is the promise made in verse 22?

Who rose first (v. 23)?

Who will rise second at Christ's coming (v. 23)?

What happens next (v. 24)?

If Christ is the firstfruit of creation, who are the second fruits?

While it's truly miraculous that Jesus rose from the grave, let's remember that this is the God who spoke the world into existence, afflicted Egypt with ten terrible plagues, and parted the Red Sea. His limitless power wasn't weakened by death. Perhaps the bigger miracle is that *we* will be raised! Though sinful and broken, we will rise from our graves to be united with Christ. Like a bud on a vine promises future fruit, Christ's resurrection is the promise of our future when we will be raised with Him.

What do the following passages reveal about what our resurrected reality will be like?

John 5:28–29

Ephesians 2:1–6

1 Thessalonians 4:16–17

What emotions does this stir in you?

You've likely been celebrating the Feast of Firstfruits all of your life without realizing it. We call this feast a different name. Do you know what it is?

That's right. It's Easter!

When we study the whole Bible, we see that Easter is so much more than a celebration of Christ's resurrection. Resurrection Day is an annual rhythm of remembrance that because Jesus lives forever, we will too.

Why do you think Paul concluded his practical letter on how to live the Christian life by focusing on the resurrection?

How does this resurrection hope impact the way you live your daily life?

THE BEST OF THE BEST

BIG IDEA: *Jesus is worthy of our very best.*

READ LEVITICUS 27:30

When was the last time someone gave you their very best?

I tried to come up with the answer to that question myself to start this lesson, but my mind just looked like that little thought bubble that pops up when you're waiting for someone to text you back.

Thinking . . . thinking . . . still thinking . . .

I *really* drew a blank when I tried to think of the last time *I* gave someone else my very best. The best of my time, the best of my energy, the best of my gifts. In truth, I usually hold something back, most often because I don't want to invest the energy required to give my very best. Other times, I'm restrained by scarcity, the fear that if I give my best away, I will need it back for myself.

The Feast of Firstfruits is first and foremost a reminder of the resurrection power found in Christ. But, there is another, more practical application of this feast. Because Christ is the firstfruit of all creation, He is worthy of our very best.

Head back to the description of the Feast of Firstfruits found in Leviticus 23:9–14. Unlike the Passover and the Feast of Unleavened Bread, the Israelites were not instructed to observe this feast immediately. *Instead, when would they begin observing the Feast of Firstfruits?*

This represents a pivot in the Seven Feasts.

While Passover and the Feast of Unleavened Bread were instituted in Egypt, the land of slavery, the Feast of Firstfruits was the beginning of additional feasts to be celebrated in the Promised Land. In Egypt, the crops of God's people belonged, humanly speaking, to Pharaoh. But, these were now free people, their lives were their own. God used the Feast of Firstfruits to teach them how to dedicate their lives back to Him.

Let's list the steps of this feast.

Step 1: _____ the harvest (v. 10).

Step 2: Bring the _____ of the _____ of the harvest to the priest (v. 10).

Step 3: He shall _____ the _____ before the _____ (v. 11) on the day after the _____ (v. 11).

Step 4: So that you may be _____ (v. 11).

Step 5: On the day when you _____ _____ _____, you shall offer a _____ ____ a year old without blemish as a burnt offering to the Lord (v. 12).

Step 6: And the _____ _____ with it shall be two tenths of an _____ of _____ flour mixed with oil, a _____ _____ to the Lord with a pleasing aroma (v. 13).

Step 7: And the _____ _____ with it shall be of _____, a fourth of a hin (v. 13).

Step 8: And you shall eat neither _____ nor _____ parched or fresh until this same day, until you have brought the offering of your God (v. 14).

List the specific offerings, or gifts, God's people were instructed to give to Him for this feast. Next to each offering, write any descriptive words given in the text.

What is similar about these offerings?

Let's circle back to Exodus 12 again. Write down the instructions given for the offering in the first Passover (Ex. 12:5).

Reach back in your memory all the way to Week Two. *The Passover lamb was to be blemish-free because he was a picture of whom?*

Yes! The offering was to be perfect because it was a picture of Jesus Christ, our perfect, spotless Lamb. Here in the Feast of Firstfruits the quality of the offering matters once again because of what it symbolizes.

Jesus gave us His firstfruits. The very best He had to offer in His death for our behalf, His resurrection and triumph over sin, and the beautiful promise that we will rise with Him.

We return our firstfruits to Him, the very best we have to offer, as both a picture of who Christ is and an act of worship, expressing that He is worthy.

READ ACTS 17:24-25
Did God need the grain, meat, or wine He required of the Israelites?

God didn't require the grain, meat, and wine offerings because He was hungry. The Feasts were about reminding God's people who God was. He was revealing His heart, not filling His stomach. In the Feast of Firstfruits, God revealed His heart to give His children His very best, Jesus. He also taught us to dedicate our very best to Him in return as an act of worship.

Throughout Scripture, we see the principle of the tithe, giving back to God a percentage of the wealth He's given us. God's instructions on tithing are very clear (Lev. 27:30–33; Num. 18:26; Deut. 14:22; Matt. 6:1–4) because He knows our sinful tendencies to both forget His benefits and grab on to the good things for ourselves.

Based on what you know about human nature and your own heart, what kind of grain and livestock might God's people have given as offerings if God did not specifically call for their best?

Circle the areas below where you are tempted to give God your second best.

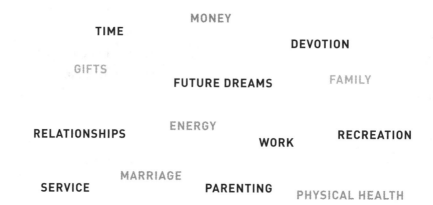

MONEY

TIME

DEVOTION

GIFTS

FUTURE DREAMS   FAMILY

ENERGY

RELATIONSHIPS   RECREATION

WORK

MARRIAGE

SERVICE   PARENTING   PHYSICAL HEALTH

At the Feast of Firstfruits, the Israelites were required to give God their very best. The worthiness of Christ requires us to do the same. God doesn't need our grain or our gifts. He needs neither our dollars nor our dreams for the future. We offer these things to Him as a way of posturing our hearts. We give our best to the Lord, not the leftovers, because He gave His best to us, *Himself.*

Conclude today's study by praying through the list of priorities in the word cloud above, asking the Lord to reveal where you've given Him your seconds, rather than firstfruits. Tell Him your desire to worship Him with your best and ask Him to help. Because He always gives us our best, He will surely do it.

BRINGING IN THE SHEAVES

BIG IDEA: *The gospel changes why we give God our best.*

READ MATTHEW 6:33

Hi, my name is Erin and I'm a workaholic.

I'm a Type AA first-born achiever who naturally gravitates toward the idols of perfectionism and achievement. In my flesh, I tend to overvalue productivity and projects and undervalue people and God's presence.

I hope that if you were among those who know me well, you would not characterize me this way. That's not because I'm hiding my true self. I'll tell anyone who will listen that I'm a frequent passenger on the Hot Mess Express. Yet Christ has done a wonderful work in me. Though I never do it perfectly, God's Word has shown me how to turn from the idols of perfection and performance and toward the everyday worship of Christ more and more.

Maybe you've sung the old hymn, Bringing in the Sheaves, before. The lyrics point to the Feast of Firstfruits and go like this . . .

Bringing in the sheaves, bringing in the sheaves,
We shall come rejoicing, bringing in the sheaves,
Bringing in the sheaves, bringing in the sheaves,
We shall come rejoicing, bringing in the sheaves.[12]

Look back at Leviticus 23:9–14. What were the Israelites to do with the sheaves of grain they collected?

According to verse 11, what was dependent upon this practice?

I don't know about you, but if I feel like God's acceptance of me is dependent on my actions, I struggle to rejoice as I obey. Instead, I resist or default to legalism. I obey with a stubborn or anxious heart. The things God requires of me, such as serving the church, forgiving others, and learning God's Word become drudgery rather than a delight.

If I get spiritual amnesia about my acceptance by Christ, I can easily read a Bible study lesson like the one we completed yesterday, and start beating myself up about all the ways I'm not giving God my best. This is why we cannot revisit the gospel too often.

Read Ephesians 1:3–14. Underline everything that is already ours "in him."

In the Old Testament, God's people gave God their best to earn His acceptance. We live in a New Testament reality in which we give God our best because we're already accepted. We've shifted from works to worship.

This is good news for those of us who struggle with perfectionism. (I'm looking at you, dear reader). We are free to bring in the sheaves . . .

Of our time . . .

Of our talent . . .

Of our finances . . .

Of everything . . . with rejoicing hearts knowing that we are fully loved, fully saved, and fully accepted by Jesus already.

In what areas of your life are you trying to earn God's acceptance?

In what areas are you most motivated by worship for all He's already done?

When we have a day where God gets the crumbs of our time and energy, we don't wilt. We repent, believe the gospel, and ask God to empower us to give our best tomorrow.

You likely already know Jesus' words found in Matthew 6:33. *Read them again and write them below.*

What is Jesus reminding us to do?

Let's practice widening the lens. Look up Matthew 6:31. What heart issue was Jesus addressing when He told us to seek the Kingdom first?

God-first living isn't meant to cause anxiety. In fact, it's the antidote. "Seek first the Kingdom" is a way of life that flows from a heart grateful for the best things God has given us. When we have the hope of the gospel as our center, we are free to give God our best with happy hearts.

Conclude today's study by reading the story of a woman who gave God her best found in Luke 21:1–4.

3 QUESTIONS FOR GROUP STUDY

1. What does this tell us about God?

2. What does this tell us about us?

3. How should we respond?

The Feast of Weeks

I don't know the difference between a spark plug and a transmission, but I do know that when it comes to cars, more power is better than less. Put any of us behind the wheel and we want something that will go, preferably fast. No one wants to putter from Point A to Point B, restricted by the powerlessness of a wimpy engine.

This same principle applies to our spiritual lives. We don't want weak, wimpy faith that moves us closer to Jesus with the power of a weed eater. We want turbo engines, lives that roar with the power of God.

In Acts 1:8, Jesus promised, "But you will receive power when the Holy Spirit has come upon you, and you will be my witnesses in Jerusalem and in all Judea and Samaria, and to the end of the earth."

It is the Holy Spirit who empowers us to live lives that showcase the goodness of God. Without Him, you and I have about as much power as a dead battery, a stalled engine, or a barely-there breeze.

This week as we examine the Feast of Weeks, may you grow in gratitude for the power given to you by the Holy Spirit and rest knowing God always does all the heavy lifting.

HOPE FOR THOSE WHO WAIT

BIG IDEA: *God is at work in seasons of waiting.*

READ ISAIAH 40:31; PSALM 27:13–14; LAMENTATIONS 3:25

I'm going to make an assumption about you: you don't like to wait.

I haven't been spying on you. Scout's honor. I haven't actually witnessed you anxiously tapping your fingers in the car pick-up line or heard your deep sighs in the grocery store checkout. I have noticed that most of us hate to wait, which is odd considering we've had so much practice.

While the first three feasts occur back-to-back, the fourth feast comes after a long season of waiting. When I'm waiting on the Lord, especially when the wait is long, my spiritual amnesia often flares up. The Feast of Weeks jogs our memory about the faithfulness of God, pointing forward through history to the moment that proves the best things come to those who wait.

Let's take a look at some significant periods of waiting recorded in Scripture, starting with our familiar friends, the Israelites. By the time the Seven Feasts were put in place, they had lots of practice waiting for the Lord.

Write down any examples that come to mind.

This pattern of waiting began with Israel's patriarch, Abraham.

What promise did God give Abram (later Abraham) in Genesis 12:1–3?

According to Genesis 12:4, how old was Abram when God made him this promise?

According to Genesis 21:5, how old was Abraham when his son Isaac was born?

How many years did he have to wait?

Is there anything in your life you've been waiting on the Lord for more than 20 years? **Write about it below.** *What are you waiting for the Lord to do? What encourages you as you wait? What discourages you?*

Joseph also knew a thing or two about waiting.

According to Genesis 37:2, how old was Joseph right before his brothers sold him into slavery?

We know from Scripture that Joseph was a God-fearing boy. Surely he began crying out to the Lord for deliverance as soon as the shackles of slavery were slapped onto his wrists, but his rescue was not quick (in human terms). Though temporarily elevated within Potiphar's household, he soon found himself enslaved and imprisoned and . . . *still waiting* for God to set him free.

Eventually God used a dream to save Joseph from the Egyptian prison and elevate him to a position of power. This would set the stage for much of what we've studied. *According to Genesis 41:46, how old was Joseph when God finally moved him from prisoner to person of influence?*

Is there anything you've been waiting on the Lord for since childhood?

Another character in the Bible that knew what it was like to wait is Daniel. A mysterious passage that has always captured my imagination is found in Daniel 10:12–14. *Read it below.*

> Then he said to me, "Fear not, Daniel, for from the first day that you set your heart to understand and humbled yourself before your God, your words have been heard, and I have come because of your words. The prince of the kingdom of Persia withstood me twenty-one days, but Michael, one of the chief princes, came to help me, for I was left there with the kings of Persia, and came to make you understand what is to happen to your people in the latter days. For the vision is for days yet to come."

What questions does this passage stir up in you?

The "he" in this passage is a heavenly messenger (10:2–6) who tells Daniel that Daniel's prayers were immediately answered. *But how many days before Daniel knew it?*

Why was Daniel forced to wait?

What prayers are you waiting for the Lord to answer right now?

Does it comfort you to know that help is already on the way?

The worst season of waiting in human history occurs between Malachi 4:6 and Matthew 1:1.

Write down each of those verses, placing an ellipsis (. . .) between the two.

The gap between the Old and New Testaments represents a four-hundred-year span that I consider the darkest years in human history. God's Word is silent. The prophets stopped prophesying. God's people were scattered.

And yet, God was at work in the ellipsis. His redemptive plan was moving forward, even if human eyes could not see it.

Read the instructions given to the Israelites for the Feast of Weeks recorded in Leviticus 23:15–22.

How many days were the Israelites instructed to wait between the sheaf of the wave offering and the beginning of the Feast of Weeks?

This feast begins with a season of counting. This feast is called the Feast of Weeks because God's people were instructed to meticulously count the days and weeks between feasts.

I imagine week one went great. God's people had just celebrated His generosity in the Feast of Firstfruits. The harvest was plentiful and God's care was evident. Weeks two and three might have flown by the same way. I wonder if my familiar companions Discouragement and Doubt made an appearance in week four? When life goes on, day after day, week after week—without rhythms of remembrance—it's too easy to forget who God is. Weeks five and six might have brought Fear and Defeat. By the time week seven arrived, nearly two months had passed since God's people had gathered to celebrate His work in their lives.

And yet, even in the waiting, even when our hearts are faint, and our prayers seem unanswered, even in the ellipses . . . God is at work. Help is already on the way. As we'll see in the days ahead, *God never wastes the wait.*

Conclude today's study by reflecting on Hebrews 10:23–24. Consider the areas of waiting you listed in today's study. How can you hold fast to hope as you wait?

TWO NEON ARROWS

BIG IDEA: *All of the Old Testament points forward to Christ's coming. All of the New Testament points backwards toward the cross.*

READ 2 CORINTHIANS 1:20

I met with Rabbi Lane at Starbucks. He brought his Torah and I brought my Bible. For hours we compared notes over steaming drinks. I'll be honest: his knowledge of Scripture put mine to shame. Though he is a devout Jew and I am a committed Christian, our hearts were united over one thing: our love for the Word of God.

"Christians don't read the book of Leviticus," I told him.

"That's rather strange and ironic," he replied.

"You think so?"

"Yes, because the idea of sacrifice is so central to Christianity. That's not exclusively, but primarily, what the book of Leviticus is about," he said.

The Torah is made up of the first five books of the Bible. *List the first five books below.*

What book is in the middle of the Torah?

"And so Jewish tradition says it's the heart and soul of the Torah," Rabbi Lane explained. "And that's partly a spatial issue, but it's also intellectual, psychological, spiritual. So if Leviticus is central, then the question becomes, 'What's Leviticus really all about?' And I think what it's ultimately all about is trying to understand the relationship that human beings can have with God."

As Christians, we look to another place in Scripture as the central pivot point: the Gospels. As we learn to look for Jesus in the Seven Feasts, we are developing muscles that help us as we study all of Scripture.

Using the chart below, outline what you know about the differences between the Old Testament and the New Testament.

THE OLD TESTAMENT	THE NEW TESTAMENT
Example: Written before Christ	Written after Christ
Focus on the sacrificial system	Focus on Christ's sacrifice

When you think of your own approach to Scripture, do you tend to gravitate more toward the Old Testament or the New?

What words would you use to describe God as He is portrayed in the Old Testament?

What words would you use to describe God as He is portrayed in the New Testament?

Do you see these testaments as complementary, in conflict, or both? Explain.

My own study of God's Word has been transformed as I've learned to see these testaments as two neon arrows: one (the Old Testament) pointing *forward* toward Jesus and one (the New Testament) pointing *backward* toward Jesus.

The feasts are a prime example. What have you learned about Jesus and the gospel so far through this study of the Seven Feasts?

If Leviticus 23 was just an old list of rules for the ancient Israelites, this would be a short and tedious study. Memorizing outdated information is boring, and I would have lost your attention early on in Week One. But Leviticus 23 is so much more! As we've studied so far, the Seven Feasts are rhythms given by God to showcase His character and redemptive plan.

The Old Testament is jam-packed with God's promises. Here are a few of my favorites found in the book of Leviticus.

Jot down what the Bible promises in the passages below.

Leviticus 26:11–12

Leviticus 26:4–5

Leviticus 26:9

Leviticus 26:42

Write out 2 Corinthians 1:20.

How do the promises you outlined above find their "yes" in Jesus and His gospel?

While God did keep His promises immediately to the nation of Israel described in the Old Testament, He also used their story to point forward to the moment when His covenant promises would be kept for us through Christ.

Think back to the institution of the Lord's Supper from Week Three. What did Jesus tell His disciples the wine and unleavened bread symbolized? (Mark 14:22–24)

Read and interact with Hebrews 7:11–28.

Underline verse 11.

Circle the descriptions of the Old Testament priests.

Double underline the descriptions of Jesus as priest.

If the descriptions of priests found in the Old Testament (mostly in the book of Leviticus) don't apply to us, who could blame us for avoiding that section of Scripture entirely? But they do! They point forward to a new, better priest—to *our* Priest, Jesus Christ!

Lean in. Listen very closely.

The Old Testament is about Jesus. The New Testament is about Jesus. (Just like my life is about Jesus and your life is about Jesus.)

When we learn to view Scripture through the gospel lens, it changes everything. Rather than the puzzle pieces of the Bible feeling scattered and discombobulated, they start to connect. The pieces fit together to seamlessly showcase God's character and His redemptive plan.

Let's practice viewing God's Word through the gospel grid by looking again at the Seven Feasts.

What important New Testament event occurred on Passover? (Hint: the answer is found in Week Two, Day Five.)

What important New Testament event occurred on the Feast of Unleavened Bread? (Hint: the answer is found in Week Three, Day Five.)

What important New Testament event occurred on the Feast of Firstfruits? (Hint: The answer is found in Week Four, Day Two.)

Wrap up today's study by reflecting on what pieces of the puzzle have become clearer to you through this study.

What have you learned about the character of God?

What have you learned about God's redemptive plan?

PENTECOST

BIG IDEA: *The Feast of Weeks points forward to Pentecost, when the Holy Spirit was poured out on the church.*

READ ACTS 1:1–2:12

Anyone who thinks that Christians are boring has never read about Pentecost. With tongues of fire, sounds of rushing winds, and a band of disciples suddenly able to speak in other languages, Pentecost is among the least boring moments in human history.

Perhaps the Holy Spirit seems like a New Testament addition to the Trinity, like the Father and the Son added a third member to the band after centuries as a duo. The Feast of Weeks shows us that the Holy Spirit has always been an essential member of the Godhead. His presence in our lives has always been a part of God's redemptive plan.

As you read about Pentecost in Acts 1 and 2, what questions come to mind?

Let's widen the lens and look at the big picture of the book of Acts for a moment. Acts is the second in a two-part series of letters, both written to Theophilus. Part one is the Book of Luke, outlining the events of Christ's life and death. Part two is the Book of Acts, which describes the birth of the church. If the book of Luke is the "what," the book of Acts is the "so what?" or the "what next?," showcasing how the gospel immediately began to change the world.

Here's a race through the events leading up to this book:

- Christ was born as a baby and raised by Mary and Joseph.
- He rounded up a team of disciples and together they ignited a spiritual and political firestorm.
- He was falsely accused by religious leaders, tried, crucified, and buried.
- Three days later He rose from the grave in triumph over sin, death, and the powers of darkness.

Jesus once again walked the earth, appearing to many. Fill in the chart outlining who Jesus appeared to after the resurrection.

REFERENCE	WHO DID JESUS APPEAR TO?	WHAT DID JESUS SAY?
John 20:14–16	Mary Magdalene	"Woman, why are you weeping? Whom are you seeking?", "Mary!"
Matthew 28:9–10		
Luke 24:34		

REFERENCE	WHO DID JESUS APPEAR TO?	WHAT DID JESUS SAY?
Luke 24:13–16		
John 20:19–24	The disciples, minus Thomas	"Peace be with you."
John 20:26–29	The disciples, Simon Peter, Thomas (Didymus), Nathanael, the sons of Zebedee, two others.	
John 21:1–2		
Matthew 28:16–17		

According to Acts 1:3, how long did Jesus remain on earth following His resurrection?

According to Acts 1:4, where did Jesus instruct His disciples to wait?

According to Acts 1:4–5, what (or Who) were they waiting for?

According to Acts 1:8, how would this promise change their lives?

Though Christ had triumphed over sin on the cross and defeated death at the resurrection, the disciples still had to wait for some of the promises of God to be fulfilled, primarily the arrival of the Holy Spirit.

When they asked Jesus how long they would have to wait, how did Jesus respond (v. 7)?

Do you think this answer satisfied their need to know? Why or why not?

Jesus was pointing out both His omniscience (that He knows all) and His sovereignty (that He rules over all). *Are the omniscience and sovereignty of God a comfort to you as you wait? Explain.*

Acts 2:1 describes the day the disciples were filled with the Holy Spirit as the Day of Pentecost. Without understanding the Seven Feasts, we could easily miss when this occurred on God's redemptive calendar. The word "Pentecost" means "50" in Greek. That number should ring a bell.

Let's think back. *How many days were the Israelites instructed to wait between the sheaf of the wave offering and the beginning of the Feast of Weeks?*

Bingo!

While the disciples were gathered in Jerusalem because of Jesus' command, on this specific day, they were gathered for an additional reason, to observe the Feast of Weeks.

Marvel again at how the events that make up the core of our faith occurred in perfect timing with the Seven Feasts.

Jesus died on Passover.

He rested on the Sabbath.

He rose on the Feast of Firstfruits.

He sent the Holy Spirit on the Feast of Weeks/Pentecost. (Is this stuff still blowing your mind? It is still blowing mine. God's Word is such a deep well!)

While the Holy Spirit was poured out on Christ's followers at Pentecost, He was always present and active with the Father and the Son.

Here are a few of the glimpses we get of the Holy Spirit in the Old Testament.

- The Holy Spirit participated in creation (Gen. 1:2; Job 26:13).
- The Holy Spirit was active in the lives of judges, warriors, and prophets throughout the Old Testament including Joshua (Num. 27:18), Gideon (Judg. 6:34), Saul (1 Sam. 10:9–10), Ezekiel (Ezek. 2:2), and King David (2 Sam. 23:2).

- God removed the Holy Spirit from King Saul (1 Sam. 16:14). David feared the same punishment because of his sin and prayed, "take not your Holy Spirit from me" (Ps. 51:11).

Where else do you see evidence of the Holy Spirit at work in the Old Testament?

It was the *Old Testament* prophet Joel who announced, "And it shall come to pass afterward, that I will pour out my Spirit on all flesh; your sons and your daughters shall prophesy, your old men shall dream dreams, and your young men shall see visions. Even on the male and female servants in those days I will pour out my Spirit" (Joel 2:28–29).

God had long ago promised that the magnificent gift of the Holy Spirit was coming, even pointing forward to Pentecost through The Feast of Weeks, but God's people had to wait between the promise and the gift.

What would have happened if the disciples had grown impatient in waiting for God's promise, stopped waiting, and abandoned their post in Jerusalem? What would they have missed?

We live in the waiting too. While Christ has given us so much, many of His promises won't be realized until He returns again for us, His bride. (More on that in our next week!) He has mercifully given us a Helper, the Holy Spirit, to guide us as we wait.

Cry out to the Lord now. Tell Him what promises you are struggling to wait for. Ask the Holy Spirit to guide and comfort you while you wait.

LIFE IN THE SPIRIT

BIG IDEA: *The Holy Spirit empowers us to live as God calls us to.*

READ GALATIANS 5:16

"I don't know how you do it."

I never know how to take that remark whenever it is thrown my way.

Is it a compliment? Kind of a round about way of saying "I'm impressed by you"? Is it a dig? A nicer way of saying, "You're clearly in way over your head, girl"? I can't tell. Over the years I've started giving an answer that tends to silence fans and critics alike, "I'm empowered by the Holy Spirit."

I'll admit it makes things a little awkward during small talk, but it's absolutely true. I am desperately dependent on the Holy Spirit to help me live what I read in God's Word. We have the unique privilege of living as God's children post-Pentecost. To understand the magnitude of that gift, let's head back to Leviticus 23:15–22.

List everything God's people were required to do or give in celebration of the Feast of Weeks.

The Feast of Weeks requires the most significant offering of all seven feasts. *Do you think this was a hardship for God's people? Explain.*

What does God require from us? Write down the answers found in the following passages.

Micah 6:8

Matthew 22:36–40

1 Peter 1:16

How ya doin' with that list in your own life?

Rockstar status				C is average, right?				Avoid eye contact	
1	2	3	4	5	6	7	8	9	10

If we're trying to wrap our heads around God's requirements for the believer, this is just the tip of the iceberg. To be clear, these are not commands tied to our salvation. We are saved through Christ alone, but this is how we are to live *because* of Christ's work in us.

Compared to humility, all-in love for God and others, and Christ-like holiness, an offering of lambs, goats, and bread seems easy peasy. Following Christ requires significant, daily sacrifice. We cannot do it in our flesh. Good news! We don't have to.

Draw lines connecting these verses with the true statement about the Holy Spirit. (Verses can connect to more than one statement).

John 14:26

Because of the Holy Spirit, I am a witness for Jesus.

The Holy Spirit was sent by Jesus.

John 16:7–8

The Holy Spirit is my helper.

The Holy Spirit will help me remember Jesus' commands.

1 Corinthians 2:10–11

The Holy Spirit was sent by the Father.

The Holy Spirit gives me power.

Acts 1:8

The Holy Spirit will teach me all things.

The Holy Spirit convicts the world concerning sin and righteousness and judgment.

Galatians is a New Testament epistle, written by Paul to the church in Galatia. One theme woven throughout this letter is our need to live in the guidance and power of the Holy Spirit.

Galatians is the book that gives us the Fruit of the Spirit (5:22–23). *Without peeking, can you list the Fruit of the Spirit? Give it a try!*

This list is important because these are the marks of God's people, the heart attitudes that flow out into the behaviors required by the Word. But this is not a list of do's and don'ts. Paul is clearly telling us that these are areas of our hearts that can only be transformed by the Spirit. Our flesh cannot drum up an ounce of joy, a fleck of goodness, a hint of self-control . . . we are desperately dependent on the Holy Spirit, our Helper, to grow this fruit in us.

How does Paul encourage us to walk in Galatians 5:16?

Paul is teaching us to walk in step with the Holy Spirit, not in step with our sinful flesh. The Fruit of the Spirit is actually a second list, meant to counterbalance the "fruit" of the flesh.

Record the fruit of the flesh vs. the fruit of the Spirit in the chart below.

THE FRUIT OF THE FLESH (Galatians 5:19–21)	THE FRUIT OF THE SPIRIT (Galatians 5:22–23)

Without the Holy Spirit, we will all gravitate toward the first list and move toward increasingly sinful patterns and behaviors. But we are not left to fight the flesh alone! We have the Holy Spirit who empowers us to choose the second list and grow more and more like Christ.

I hope Peter won't mind being our poster child for this truth.

Read about Peter before Pentecost in Luke 22:54–62.

Read about Peter after Pentecost in Acts 2:14–41.

What transformed Peter from a man who couldn't work up the nerve to declare Christ to a servant girl to a man who boldly declared Christ to the nations? Not what, but *Who*—the Holy Spirit.

Who will transform us from women ruled by our flesh, to women ruled by Christ? The Holy Spirit!

Who will enable us to stop our natural navel-gazing and love our neighbors as ourselves? The Holy Spirit!

Who will remind us of all God is showing us in His Word so we don't have to live in the fog of spiritual amnesia? The Holy Spirit!

Who will guide and protect us as we count the weeks between now and Christ's coming? The Holy Spirit!

Let me give you a practical example. Week Three (The Feast of Unleavened Bread) was a huge struggle for me to write. I tried and tried, but over and over kept deleting the words because I knew I wasn't correctly representing all that God's Word says about sin. Days turned into weeks. My deadline edged ever closer, but I was stuck. Out of frustration, I reached out to a small circle of close friends and asked them to spend the day praying for me. (Why is prayer so often our last resort?) They faithfully prayed and the results were stunning. In a single day, I wrote more words (and better words) than I had in weeks. The spiritual and mental clog I was facing was unstuck and I was able to write with something close to effortlessness.

What shifted? My friends and I declared my need for God's power. In my own strength, I have neither the attention span nor the giftedness to write more than a few meaningful words, much less a whole book. But when I confess my weakness and ask the Lord for help, He gives it, in heaping portions.

Maybe you don't write books. But do you need to love people who are hard to love? Do you work a job that sometimes feels impossible or boring? Are you the momma of children you don't know how to raise, the wife of a husband you don't know how to love, the neighbor of a family you don't know how to serve? Then you need the Spirit's power too. Your limited abilities and resources will never be enough.

How do we do it all? Simply put, we don't. We keep our feet on the path of obedience and depend desperately on the Holy Spirit to help us with the rest.

End today's study by considering Romans 8:14, "For all who are led by the Spirit of God are sons of God."

Ask a trusted friend what evidence she sees of the Holy Spirit at work in your life.

THE HEARTBEAT OF OUR SABBATH

BIG IDEA: *When we Sabbath, we showcase our dependence on God.*

READ COLOSSIANS 1:16–18

I like the hearts and flowers of Valentine's Day, the leprechaun of St. Patrick's Day, and the harvest table settings of Thanksgiving as much as the next girl, but as the years fly by, I grow increasingly hungry for rhythms of remembrance that focus on Christ. Year after year, as I gather my children, my family, and my friends around my table for various holidays, I want them to walk away with a renewed awareness of the goodness of God, not the merit of my centerpieces.

Maybe, as you've studied the feasts you've felt a longing for new rhythms too. As new covenant Christians, we aren't required to give up leaven, bring the firstfruits of our harvest to the priest, or sacrifice sheep and goats. Yet there are many ways we can infuse the heart of the Seven Feasts into our weeks, our years, our lives. The most obvious of which is a commitment to Sabbath.

You may be thinking, "Didn't we already learn about Sabbath, way back in Week One, then again in Week Four?" I'm so glad you were paying attention. We did indeed. But we honor the rhythm of the Seven Feasts by looking at Sabbath once again.

Skim back through the descriptions of the Seven Feasts outlined in Leviticus 23:3–44. Write down all commands to Sabbath.

Exactly how many feasts include Sabbath?

Based on what you've learned about Sabbath and the feasts so far, why do you think God included this commandment so often?

READ 1 SAMUEL 21:1–6

Again the book of Leviticus helps us understand the other 65 pieces of the puzzle. *According to Leviticus 24:5–9, who was allowed to eat the holy bread?*

"Aaron and his sons" refers to the priests. This bread was to be reserved for priests only.

Ahimelech the priest wasn't just prying into David's army's bedroom affairs. Sexual contact would have made them unclean (Lev. 15:18), not to mention the fact that they were not priests. This was a violation of the *letter* of the law, but was it a violation of the *spirit* of the law? That brings us back to Sabbath.

READ MATTHEW 12:1–8
What did Jesus do on the Sabbath (v. 1)?

What did the Pharisees accuse Jesus' disciples of (v. 2)?

Did this violate the "rules" for Sabbath outlined in the Seven Feasts?

Jesus points out to the religious leaders that David violated Levitical law by eating the holy bread, yet he was not condemned. Similarly, the priests, in carrying out their duties, had to work on the Sabbath but were "guiltless" (v. 5).

Write down Christ's words recorded in verse 6–7.

Circle the phrase "something greater."

Write down Christ's words recorded in verse 8. Draw a line from these words to the phrase you circled above.

The Pharisees were so caught up in the rules of the Sabbath, they missed the Lord of the Sabbath. The purpose of Sabbath is to point to Jesus, not to rules or rituals.

Like you, I live with an ever-growing to-do list. To take a break from my work, even for a single day, means I run the risk of an inbox so full I'll never find the bottom and a laundry pile so high I will never find the top. And yet, work in my own strength can never achieve what I want it to, anyway. I need the help of the Holy Spirit to honor Christ with my work, my home, my family, and my relationships. Regular rhythms of Sabbath showcase our dependence on the Lord.

What is Sabbath, at its very core? Write down what each of the following verses teach us.

1. Sabbath is a time for. . . (Ex. 16:23)

2. Sabbath is a time to. . . (Matt. 12:12)

3. The Sabbath was made to benefit. . . (Mark 2:27)

Adding Sabbath to your calendar as one more thing to do, one more hoop to try to jump through, will not honor the heart of the Bible or the Seven Feasts. We can, however, honor the Lord of the Sabbath when we change the pattern and rest in His power.

Why not start today? Today's lesson is intentionally short to allow you time for two things:

1. Look at your calendar for the coming months. Block out a weekly Sabbath and commit to lay aside your work to rest in Christ's work each week.

2. Develop Sabbath muscles by resting for a moment at the conclusion of this week's study. No lists to make. No boxes to check. Just rest in the truth that the unmatched power of God doesn't depend on you.

3 QUESTIONS FOR GROUP STUDY

1. What does this tell us about God?

2. What does this tell us about us?

3. How should we respond?

The Feast of Trumpets

Consider the story of Abraham and Isaac found in Genesis 22:1–14.

God asked Abraham to sacrifice his beloved son, a foreshadowing of the moment when God the Father would send His one and only Son to die on our behalf. In Abraham's case, his son was spared. God mercifully provided a sacrificial ram instead.

> And Abraham lifted up his eyes and looked, and behold, behind him was a ram, caught in a thicket by his horns. And Abraham went and took the ram and offered it up as a burnt offering instead of his son. (v. 13)

This week, we will study the moment when human history comes to its final crescendo as recorded in Revelation 11:15:

> Then the seventh angel blew his trumpet, and there were loud voices in heaven, saying, "The kingdom of the world has become the kingdom of our Lord and of his Christ, and he shall reign forever and ever."

As we picture the trumpet blasts described throughout the Bible, our mind may naturally envision our modern, metal trumpet. More likely, God's people blew a shofar, or ram's horn. From Genesis to Revelation, God uses the horn to declare His salvation. The trumpet blast on the Day of the Lord will be a pronouncement that God's people are saved from death and sin once and for all.

Jesus observed many of the Seven Feasts during His time on earth, but not the Feast of Trumpets. At least, *not yet.*

One day soon Jesus will fulfill the Feast of Trumpets with His triumphant return. As you study the fifth feast this week, may you long for His second coming and learn to listen, with great expectation, for the blast of the final trumpet.

TRUMPETS AND THE POWER AND PRESENCE OF THE LORD

BIG IDEA: *In the Bible trumpets symbolize the power and presence of the Lord.*

READ EXODUS 19

It's the spouse sitting next to you absorbed in his phone . . .

It's the co-worker so consumed by her own assignments she fails to see your contribution . . .

It's the friend so busy listening to the sound of her own voice she never takes a breath to hear from you . . .

We all know what it's like to be with someone and still miss their presence.

I face this temptation most often with my children. I'm physically with my children for hours every day, but most often I'm too busy loading dishwashers, packing lunches, and picking up dirty laundry to look into their little eyes. Like little warning sirens, their temper tantrums alert me that they don't care if the dishes are clean. They want my undivided attention, my presence.

As we explore the Feast of Trumpets together, we'll see that the Bible uses trumpets as a symbol of many things, including God's powerful presence.

Open your Bible again to Exodus 19. Before we dig in, let's practice looking for context. This chapter represents a significant pivot in the Book of Exodus. Up until this point, the book has recorded the oppression and liberation of Israel.

According to Exodus 19:1, where are the Israelites now?

Start with what you know. Does anything bubble up in your memory about Mount Sinai?

The second half of the book is not set in Egypt where the Israelites had been enslaved, or on their earliest days in transition to free people. The rest of the book is set at Mt. Sinai and focuses on the Lord revealing His covenant through Moses.

Exodus 20 gets lots of attention from Bible scholars and teachers alike, so it may already be familiar to you. *What happens in Exodus 20?*

The handing down of the Ten Commandments is a significant event, but if we skip past the preceding chapter, we miss the drama of what God was doing.

Circle back to Exodus 19:1. What information do we get about the timing of these verses?

With 29.5 days between new moons, this puts their arrival at Sinai about seven weeks after the exodus.

What feast was celebrated on the day of the Exodus?

What feast occurs seven weeks after the Passover?

Israel's arrival at Mount Sinai coincides with the Feast of Weeks. Last week, we learned that the Feast of Weeks points forward to the pouring out of the Holy Spirit at Pentecost. Here, we see God's Spirit showcased by His awe-inspiring power.

In verses 3–6, God speaks to Moses and reveals His covenant with Israel. These verses are often called the Mosaic covenant by scholars and they complement the Abrahamic covenant given to Abraham (Gen. 12:1–3) and the new covenant given to us through Christ (Luke 22:20).

Use the chart below to fill in the specifics of the Mosaic covenant.

What did God require of Israel? (v. 5)	What did God promise Israel in return? (vv. 5–6)

How did God's people respond to the covenant? Write down their words (v. 8).

In response, how did God promise to reveal Himself to Moses (v. 9)?

Read verses 10–15. What words would you use to describe what the mood must have been like among the Israelites?

Read and interact with verse 16 below.

Underline any day and time references.

Circle what God's people saw.

Draw an arrow to what God's people heard.

Highlight how God's people reacted.

> **On the morning of the third day there were thunders and lightnings and a thick cloud on the mountain and a very loud trumpet blast, so that all the people in the camp trembled.** (ESV)

God forewarned His people that His presence would alarm them. Because He is holy, they could visit the mountain while His Spirit descended only under the strictest of orders. *According to verses 14 and 15, how did they prepare?*

The cleansing of clothes and avoidance of sexual contact were outer expressions of their heart commitment to follow God's law to be *holy*. By consecrating the Israelites, Moses was setting them apart for the sacred purpose of seeing God.

According to verse 13, what was the signal that they were to move toward God's presence on the mountain?

For the sinner, God's presence is a scary place to be.

Read Genesis 3:8. Why did Adam and Eve hide from the presence of God?

Likewise, God's people in Exodus 19 had to be cleansed, right down to their garments, because there is no place for filth in God's presence. For those of us who have been cleansed by Christ, the presence of God is an extraordinary gift.

Look up the following passages. What does each record about what is found in God's presence?

Exodus 33:14

Psalm 16:11

Psalm 31:19–20

Compare and contrast Psalm 139:7 and Matthew 28:20b below. What do these verses teach us about the presence of God?

> Where shall I go from your Spirit?
>   Or where shall I flee from your presence? (Ps. 139:7)

> And behold, I am with you always, to the end of the age. (Matt. 28:20b)

End today's study by reading Isaiah's account of entering God's presence recorded in Isaiah 6:1–4. When you consider the presence of God, what emotions are stirred up within you?

TRUMPETS AND TRIUMPH

BIG IDEA: *In the Bible trumpets symbolize God's triumph.*

READ JOSHUA 6

When we were trying to sell our little house (the one Miss Sharon delivered sourdough bread to), I tried an unusual tactic.

I grabbed the chubby fingers of my two toddler sons (the second half of Team Davis had not yet been born), and I marched around our house seven times, praying out loud for God to bring us buyers. If any neighbors peeped through their blinds, they surely thought I had lost my marbles. Perhaps they were grateful for the "for sale" sign in the front yard.

All I knew was that marching in circles had worked once before. I missed the part where the walking was meant to showcase the power of God, not to attract potential home buyers. The story found in Joshua 6 is a famous one, a favorite among Sunday school teachers everywhere. But look again at this familiar account. This time listen for the trumpet blasts.

While Joshua 6 certainly works as a stand alone story, the details take on more depth when we take the time to survey the surrounding chapters and verses.

According to Joshua 1:1, this book begins after what significant event?

What assignment did God give to Joshua (vv. 2–9)?

While his predecessor Moses had served as a shepherd, leading the Israelites out of slavery and through four decades of wilderness wandering, Joshua was more like a general. His assignment was to lead God's people in defeating the tribes who inhabited the Promised Land.

Read Joshua 5:10–12. What two feasts did the Israelites observe in Canaan?

According to verse 10, they observed these feasts in the plains of what city?

The book of Joshua doesn't fill in many details about Jericho, yet even without knowing the size of the city, we can picture the heart condition of God's people as they camped at the city's base. These were not warriors! They were slaves turned nomads who had been walking and camping for forty years, not training and fighting. Sure, God had promised to give them the victory, but presumably not without a fight. It's moments like these that our spiritual amnesia tends to kick in.

Scripture doesn't tell us if they doubted God in this moment, but it does record the observance of the first two feasts. This is what the feasts were for, to remind God's people of His character and empower them to continue to trust and obey.

As Joshua was assessing the situation, he met an angelic messenger. *Write down the angel's words to Joshua (vv. 14–15).*

With a firm commitment to obeying the Word of the Lord and an angelic being as his second in command, Joshua was emboldened to take on the city of Jericho and secure his first Promised Land victory for the people of God. The Lord employed an unusual plan of attack.

Write down the specific instructions given to the Israelites in each verse.

Joshua 6:3

Joshua 6:4

Joshua 6:5

Scripture doesn't record that Joshua argued or that he even hesitated. God said march, blow trumpets, and shout, and Joshua said, "Go forward" (v. 7).

In the middle of writing this study, I was on the team for a large conference. As writing and conference planning deadlines converged, I had one week blocked off to work the extra long hours that I thought would be required to make both projects a success. The problem is, every time I sat down at my computer to write or plan, I had the overwhelming urge to walk and pray.

While my to-do list seemed important, I was reminded that my self-sufficient attempts to make things happen with extra applications of elbow grease don't ultimately work. So all week long I walked and prayed. Tasks that seemed paramount either got done in the margin or not at all. God used the conference to impact many lives, including my own, and the fact that you are reading these words is evidence that the writing did eventually get done. The victory wasn't secured by powering through or hustling harder. *The battle was won in prayer.*

Has God ever instructed you to secure the victory in a way that seemed unusual? How did you respond?

In Joshua 6, the sound of a certain instrument would be the signal that God had given His people the victory. *What instrument was it?*

Can you think of a time when you heard a trumpet blast and the sound was particularly beautiful or moving? Write about it below.

Read and interact with Joshua 6:8–16.

Circle the word trumpet(s) *any time it appears.*

Underline all appearances of the word continually.

Draw an arrow to the word seven.

Seven trumpets blaring continually for seven days. For the people inside the walls of Jericho it must have been an intimidating sound. For God's people it was a battle cry. As long as the trumpets were blaring, their eardrums were reverberating with reminders that God was with them, He would not leave them; He would deliver their enemies into their hands.

According to verse 20, what did God's people do at the sound of the final trumpet blast?

Joshua 6 points past the life, death, and resurrection of Jesus and toward the moment when Christ will triumph over evil once and for all. It is a foreshadowing of a coming reality for *all of God's people,* not just those who watched the walls of Jericho fall.

We'll get there. I promise. For now hold these pieces of the puzzle close to your heart.

- God's people triumphed over their enemies. Not in their own power, but in God's.
- The trumpet blast was the signal the victory was won.
- Upon hearing it, the children of God entered the city and began their reign as rulers of the Promised Land.

As we wrap up today's study, let's connect a few dots between Joshua, Jericho, and the Seven Feasts.

What two feasts did Joshua and the Israelites observe in Canaan before the walls came a-tumblin' down?

What feast comes next?

In many ways, Jericho's fall represented the firstfruits of war. My ESV study Bible includes this note for Joshua 6.

> "As was often the case in ancient Near Eastern conquest accounts, key early conflicts are recounted in detail, while subsequent conflicts are noted more briefly. As the first city to be taken in Canaan, Jericho was to be wholly dedicated to the Lord, as a kind of symbolic "firstfruits" (cf. Lev. 23:10).[13]

Who did the plunders of war go to (v. 24)?

The pattern of the Seven Feasts continues, with Israel giving God their best, in this case the best spoils of war.

As you conclude today's study, spend time dwelling on Exodus 14:14. Consider any areas where you need the Lord to fight for you. Surrender them once again to His sovereign care.

EVEN MORE UNDIGNIFIED

BIG IDEA: *In the Bible, trumpets signal the worship of God's people.*

READ PSALM 29:2, PSALM 95:6, ISAIAH 12:5

There are moments when quiet gratitude is the right response to God's kindness toward us. There are other times when God's people need to whoop and holler in celebration of who God is.

Read the description of the Feast of Trumpets found in Leviticus 23:23–25. Write down the instructions given to the Israelites for the observance of this feast. What is unique about this feast?

What day of the year was the Feast of Trumpets to be celebrated?

This date might seem insignificant when consulting our modern calendars, but the Feast of Trumpets marked the end of one agricultural year and the beginning of another, an important pivot point. This feast evolved to become Rosh Hashanah, the Jewish New Year. In addition to a Sabbath rest and a food offering to the Lord, Israel was commanded to welcome the new year with a trumpet blast, a loud declaration of praise.

Turn to 1 Chronicles 13. When King David ordered the Ark of the Covenant to be retrieved from Kiriath-jearim where it had been stored, how did David and the Israelites specifically express their worship (v. 8)?

If you're picturing David and a few followers singing quietly, look again.

According to verse 5, who was assembled for the moving of the Ark? Revisit verse 1. How many Israelites were under David's command?

What two geographical points are mentioned in verse 5?

The Nile marked the southern border of Israel. Lebo-hamath was on the northern border, meaning this was no small operation. David didn't send a special ops force to retrieve the Ark quietly. Instead, he assembled the people from the bottom to the top of the nation. Picture their magnitude and envision them blasting their trumpets; hundreds of thousands of God's people gathered for miles and miles to declare their worship of God. What a sight! *What a sound!*

This was not the only time David would make a scene in worship. When the Ark was finally brought within the walls of Jerusalem, he ordered God's people to make noise to celebrate the goodness of God.

When his wife responded to his overt public worship with embarrassment and chastisement, what did David say? Write down his words found in 2 Samuel 6:21–22.

I like how the NIV version records David's words, "I will become even more undignified than this, and I will be humiliated in my own eyes . . ."

David was willing to look foolish in order to publicly worship God. Are you?

Has watching someone else worship ever embarrassed you? Write about that below.

Worship means to declare and celebrate who God is. We can worship God privately, behind closed doors, but throughout Scripture we see the call to worship publicly, to declare God's character in front of others.

Many of the psalms were written by David, the undignified worshipper, and contain repeated reminders to worship God.

Record what each of the following psalms teaches about how *we can worship.*

Psalm 29:2

Psalm 66:4

Psalm 95:1–6

Psalm 149:3

What does Psalm 22:3 say about the throne of God? What does this word picture reveal about the importance of our praise?

Psalm 98:6 ᴺɪᴠ points us to trumpets again as an instrument of worship. "With trumpets and the blast of the ram's horn—shout for joy before the Lᴏʀᴅ, the King."

Why do you think God's Word calls for trumpets in worship so often?

Listen to an orchestra, and you'll hear it; the trumpet stands out in a crowd. God doesn't need our instruments to be loud to reach Him, but He does seem to value bold acts of worship that can be heard far and wide.

Read 2 Chronicles 5:13. How did God respond to the sound of trumpets and singing in this passage?

While there are many ways to worship, the Bible makes it clear, God's people are to make some noise. That doesn't mean you have to compose sonatas or even sing on key, but music and worship are closely linked throughout Scripture.

How does music inspire you to declare and celebrate who God is?

The Bible isn't asking you to learn to play the trumpet, but to let your life declare the goodness and mercy of God *out loud*. Sing about Him with your friends and children. Wave your arms in wonder at all He has done. Beat the drum of His faithfulness. Dance because of His goodness.

Who do you know whose life is defined by a pattern of worship? How have you seen this lived out?

Like the other trumpets we've studied so far, those that call God's people to worship are also pointing forward to the future God has for His people. Every time we worship God, we are practicing for what's to come.

End today's study by reading Psalm 96. In your Bible, circle every instruction for how to worship God and underline every reason God is worthy of your praise.

THE FINAL TRUMPET

BIG IDEA: *A day is coming when a trumpet will signal the return of our King.*

READ 1 THESSALONIANS 4:15–17; REVELATION 11:15

I'm worn out by my pride, selfishness, and idol worship. I'm deeply grieved that my sin continues to put shrapnel into the hearts of the people I love the most—my husband and children, my friends, my fellow Christ followers. I long for the day when I can fully shed my sin nature and truly be like Christ.

It was in a state of disgust and frustration with my sin that I found myself cruising down the highway at 70 (okay, 75) miles per hour recently. My steering wheel was streaked with frustrated tears.

I cried to the Lord out loud, "When, Lord? When will I finally stop sinning and become holy like you are holy?!"

The phrase that bubbled up in my heart startled me, "In a moment."

My heart skipped a beat. I feared I was about to be hit by a semi-truck because I know that as long as I live in this body, I will remain a sinner. Sure, Christ is transforming me, little by little, but the process is long and often painful.

That night, I settled into a hotel room and dug my Bible out of my suitcase. It seemed I had heard that phrase "in a moment" somewhere before. As I flipped to 1 Corinthians 15:52, suddenly there it was, the answer to the question of when I would shift from sinner to saint: "in a moment, in the twinkling of an eye, at the last trumpet. For the trumpet will sound, and the dead will be raised imperishable, and we shall be changed."

The Feast of Trumpets was an announcement, given to God's people to declare that a bigger, better trumpet blast is coming.

Let's hover here in 1 Corinthians 15 together for a moment. To help with context, give yourself a couple of reminders.

Who wrote the book of 1 Corinthians?

Who did he write this book to?

What major themes have we studied from this book?

Chapter 15 is dedicated to one big idea: resurrection. We can divide this chapter into three major themes.

Fill in the key verse for each section in the chart below.

THE RESURRECTION OF CHRIST (1 Cor. 15:1–11) Record vv. 3–4	THE RESURRECTION OF THE DEAD (1 Cor. 15:12–34) Record v. 21	THE RESURRECTION BODY (1 Cor. 15:35–49) Record v. 42

These big ideas build on each other and are presented in order of importance.

First, Christ rose from the dead. Paul reminds us that Jesus' resurrection is of "first importance" (v. 3). Because Christ rose from the dead, *we* will rise from the dead. Remember, Jesus is the firstfruits and we are the second. And because we will rise from the dead, we will be given new bodies built for glory.

The Corinthian believers had questions about how all of this was going to work. (Thus, Paul's need to address it). Who could blame them? It's a mind-bending idea, isn't it? *What questions do you have about the resurrection? Write them down below.*

While I do have some questions about the practicalities of this moment, I mostly want to know this:

- When will it be?
- What will it be like?

We don't get to know the when. But we aren't left to wonder about what it will be like. The Bible describes the day of Christ's return in brilliant detail, when He will return again to establish a new heaven and new earth (Rev. 21:1).

Though all of the Old Testament points forward to Christ's first coming and all of the New Testament points backward to His death and resurrection, the whole Bible also points forward to the moment when God's redemptive plan is fulfilled.

Write down the description of Christ's return found in each of these prophetic books.

ISAIAH 27:13	JOEL 2:1	REVELATION 11:15

What do all three prophecies have in common?

What hope does the return of Christ offer us?

Let's compare the trumpet blasts we've studied so far with the final trumpet we'll one day hear.

What did we learn the trumpet symbolized in Exodus 19 (Day 1)?

Record Revelation 21:1–3. How will we experience the presence of God after the final trumpet?

What did we learn the trumpet symbolized in Joshua 6 (Day 2)?

Re-visit Joshua 6:5. What were God's people able to do after the sound of the trumpet blast?

Look again at Revelation 21:1–3. What city will we be able to enter following the blast of the final trumpet?

From the book of Psalms, we learned that the trumpet signals the worship of God's people. Read Revelation 10:7. What will the seventh trumpet signal? Why does this promise lead to worship by God's people?

Compared to eternity, the time between now and the blast of the final trumpet is just a blip, *a moment.* Christ is coming for His Bride, to rescue us and lead us to a place free from sin and death. Oh, how I long to hear the trumpet blast! For now, I wait and hope, grateful for this promise, "in a moment, in the twinkling of an eye, at the last trumpet. For the trumpet will sound, and the dead will be raised imperishable, and we shall be changed" (1 Cor. 15:52).

Close today's study by writing out a prayer, thanking God for His promised return.

FUTURE AMNESIA

BIG IDEA: *Our God-promised future changes our everyday reality.*

READ HEBREWS 10:19–22

Jewish tradition states that God writes every person's words, thoughts, and actions in the Book of Life. That book is then opened and examined by God on Rosh Hashanah, the Jewish New Year. The idea is that if good deeds outnumber sins for the preceding year, God will again inscribe the individual's name in the book for the year ahead. Rosh Hashanah ushers in ten days of repentance in which Jews seek to make amends for sins and commit good deeds to ensure their names are written in the book before the book is sealed again.

If our lives are not anchored in the gospel, we will naturally gravitate toward a version of this tradition, filling our days trying to be "good" enough to outpace the "bad" we've done.

Is there evidence in your life of trying to live this way? What has been the result?

Let's head back one more time to Leviticus 23:23–25. The instructions for the feast are pure and simple. Record them as a list below.

1.

2.

3.

4.

Of the four steps to this feast, which one is repeated?

When we view this feast through a gospel lens, the application is sweet and simple. We look forward with great expectation to the day of Christ's return. And we rest knowing that He has done the work to secure our place with Him. There is no need to spend our days trying to tip the scales in our direction. We will be with Christ because He has saved us, not because we could save ourselves (we can't).

But there is a Book of Life. Read the following verses and record your questions about each one.

Philippians 4:3

Revelation 3:5

Revelation 20:12

If you're achievement driven like me, these verses might cause you some anxiety. How can we know if our name is in the book? If the inscription is based on what we've done (Rev. 20:12), have we done enough? Can we *ever* do enough?

Let's pause and take a deep breath together. Ready? Breathe in. Breathe out.

Let's go back to what we know. Think about the 66-piece puzzle. If we only look at these few verses in a single book of the Bible, we will get a one-dimensional view of God, primarily focused on His judgment. It's time, once again, to widen the lens.

What do we see about God in Ephesians 2:4–6?

How about in Jeremiah 31:3?

What do you learn about Him in 1 Corinthians 1:9?

And in Revelation 4:9–11?

Certainly, God is a God who judges. But He is also a God of grace, of everlasting love, and of blinding holiness.

Buuut . . . how about that Book of Life? Is the question of your position within it still lingering in your mind?

This, friend, is why we need God's Word so desperately. When we forget all God has declared in His Word, we forget the gospel hope that is ours in Christ.

READ ROMANS 3:21-22

²¹But now the righteousness of God has been manifested apart from the law, although the Law and the Prophets bear witness to it— ²² the righteousness of God through faith in Jesus Christ for all who believe. For there is no distinction:

Underline the phrase "the righteousness of God."

Circle the phrase "through faith in Jesus Christ for all who believe."

Now draw arrows toward that phrase.

Pull out your highlighter and mark it again.

Our names are written in the Book of Life because of our faith in Jesus. On the cross, He mercifully transferred His righteousness to us. Listen intently to 2 Corinthians 5:21, "For our sake he made him to be sin who knew no sin, so that in him we might become the righteousness of God."

How is the book described in Psalm 69:28?

How is it described in Revelation 21:27?

Jesus' work changes everything about the Book of Life. It's true that names are written in the Book of Life based on works, *but it's Christ's work,* not ours, that secures our eternity.

When you're tempted to earn your salvation. Rest in this.
When you fear God has changed His mind about you. Rest in this.
When your good deeds don't come close to outweighing your sins. Rest in this.
As we wait for Christ's return, rest in this.

Jesus will come back for us.
He will fulfill His promise.
The trumpet will sound.
He will return.
And we will be His *forever.*

Spiritual amnesia can cause us to forget the gospel, but it can also cause the coming of Christ to slip from our minds. In contrast, living in light of Christ's return shifts our priorities, it steadies our resolve, and it lifts our eyes with hope.

Conclude today's study in prayer, asking the Lord to show you how to live in light of His return.

3 QUESTIONS FOR GROUP STUDY

1. What does this tell us about God?

2. What does this tell us about us?

3. How should we respond?

The Day of Atonement

Perhaps you've heard the story that Old Testament priests would tie a rope around their ankles before entering the holy of holies so that if God struck them dead, their bodies could be drug out. Gulp!

Welcome to Myth Busters, Bible edition! That little anecdote is not one we find in Scripture. There's no mention of rope-tethered ankles anywhere in God's Word. But as we study the sixth feast, we'll see that entering the holy of holies was serious business—deadly serious. One day per year, the high priest would enter the innermost corners of the tabernacle to atone for the sins of God's people. Life and death truly hung in the balance, not just for the priest, but for the entire nation of Israel.

The Day of Atonement exposed the Israelites' sin (and ours!) in ways that are uncomfortable. But Scripture promises us this, "But where sin abounded, grace abounded much more" (Rom. 5:20 NKJV). Ultimately, the Day of Atonement is not about our sin. It's a day dedicated to showcasing God's elaborate grace.

As you study the sixth feast this week, may you find yourself captivated by the mercy of God and rest fully in His grace.

A MATTER OF LIFE AND DEATH

BIG IDEA: *Our sin is deadly serious.*

READ JONAH 4

The Book of Jonah does not have a happy ending, at least not for Jonah.

The story is recorded in four short chapters in the Old Testament. Jonah was a prophet who boldly preached restoration and prosperity for the nation of Israel (2 Kings 14:23–28). When God's assignment shifted and Jonah was commissioned to preach repentance to the pagan city of Nineveh, he balked and hopped on a charter boat sailing to . . . anywhere but Nineveh.

God sent a storm and then a fish to woo Jonah to repentance. From inside the belly of that fish, Jonah prayed. *Read Jonah's prayer, recorded in Jonah 2.*

Verse 9 is especially poetic. Write it out below.

Jonah, it seems, was a man who understood the weight of his sin and the gift of God's salvation. Except, unfortunately, he didn't.

This study has already dedicated an entire lesson to the topic of sin. Sin and our resulting need for salvation have been woven tightly into every single feast. Maybe, like me, you're ready to move on to something . . . lighter. Let's face it, no one wants to talk about sin, especially if the topic is *our sin*. We prefer to race past it, to gloss over it, or make little of it. When we do, we repeat Jonah's mistake.

Developing new sacred rhythms that mirror the heart of the Seven Feasts means finding ways to regularly sit under the weight of our sin. Gospel-centered living requires it, because it is only when we face the reality of our sinfulness that we grasp our desperate need for a Savior.

As you read Jonah 4, what sin do you recognize in Jonah's life?

Are any of Jonah's sins present in your own life?

According to verses 2–3, why did Jonah want to die?

God's *mercy* toward the Ninevites made Jonah despair deeply. He wanted God to wipe out the city in wrath instead of saving its inhabitants. He set up camp outside Nineveh, hoping disaster would come even after God promised to relent (v. 5). *Perhaps the greatest indicator of how well we grasp the gravity of our own sin is our response to the sin of others.*

When we want to see someone face God's wrath, it's a clear indication that we've forgotten that we've been given dump truck loads of grace. My pastor often warns us against "Get-em-God prayers," those prayers we pray about others, asking God to inflict punishment.

Take a moment to ask the Holy Spirit to remind you of any Get-em-God prayers you've prayed. *Write down the names or initials of any individuals who come to mind. Now ask God to expose what your feelings about the sins of others reveals about your attitude toward your own sin.*

Jonah's pity party continued. According to verses 6–9, why did Jonah want to die?

What reminder does God give Jonah in verses 10–11? Write out God's words below.

Because Jonah was more concerned about a plant than he was about the citizens of Nineveh, we can know that he forgot the bedrock truth we're going to park our hearts on today—our sin is a matter of life and death.

God's full wrath on Nineveh would have meant the death of every man, woman, child, and creature who lived within Nineveh's walls.

According to verse 11, how many people would have died?

Like Jonah, it is possible for us to talk the talk of sin without grasping the wonder of our salvation. The sixth feast is the Day of Atonement, a reminder of both the reality of our sinfulness and the extravagance of God's grace.

The Day of Atonement was the most sacred day on the Israelite calendar. One day per year, the high priest would enter the Holy Place within the tabernacle to atone (or make amends for) the sins of God's people.

The guidelines of this feast are first outlined in Leviticus 16. *First, read the entire chapter and then we will break it down together. Write down any thoughts or questions that occur to you as you read.*

According to verse 2, where was Aaron, the high priest instructed to go on the Day of Atonement?

Let's pause here for a moment to compare notes. I typically study from the ESV Bible (the primary version I've quoted throughout this study). In that translation this verse says, "Tell Aaron your brother not to come at any time into the Holy Place inside the veil, before the mercy seat that is on the ark, so that he may not die."

This version confused me because it seems to indicate that Aaron could not enter the Holy Place, while the rest of the chapter is dedicated to instructions for what he should do once he is inside the Holy Place.

I suppose I could have just skipped that verse and pushed my questions aside, but through the years, I've learned not to rush past the parts of God's Word that perplex me. In this case, my questions were answered easily by comparing this verse in a few different translations. Take a minute and do the same right now. (An online Bible source like BibleGateway.com makes this easy.)

Comparing versions shows me that God's instructions weren't that Aaron couldn't go behind the curtain at any time, but rather that he couldn't go at any time he wanted. The high priest could only go behind the curtain on the Day of Atonement. This was the one and only time each year when someone was allowed near the mercy seat of God.

According to verse 2, what was so sacred about the mercy seat?

Who named this place within the temple the mercy seat (v. 2)?

God designated the most holy place within His sacred temple as a place of mercy. He could have called it the "judgment seat" or "the wrath seat." Instead, immediately as God hands down the rituals for the Day of Atonement, He establishes His intent—to show mercy to His people.

Exodus 25:17–22 records the details of the mercy seat. What words come to mind as you read this description?

Write out the following verses.

Deuteronomy 4:31

Lamentations 3:22–23

Ephesians 2:4–5

Do you tend to think of God as merciful? Explain.

The rituals for the Day of Atonement were elaborate and tedious and needed to be followed exactly. *Referencing Leviticus 16, fill in the chart below to highlight what was required. Because there is a lot to record, I've filled in some of the verses for you. (I've got your back, girl.)*

Animal sacrifices required	Cleansing rituals required	Burnt offerings required	Scapegoat ritual	Sabbath rituals
v. 3 But in this way Aaron shall come into the Holy Place: with a bull from the herd for a sin offering and a ram for a burnt offering. **v. 5** **vv. 6,11**	**v. 4** **vv. 23–24**	**vv. 12–13** And he shall take a censer full of coals of fire from the altar before the Lᴏʀᴅ, and two handfuls of sweet incense beaten small, and he shall bring it inside the veil and put the incense on the fire before the Lᴏʀᴅ, that the cloud of the incense may cover the mercy seat that is over the testimony, so that he does not die. **vv. 24–25**	**vv. 20–22**	**v. 29** **v. 31** It is a Sabbath of solemn rest to you, and you shall afflict yourselves; it is a statute forever.

Animal sacrifices required	Cleansing rituals required	Burnt offerings required	Scapegoat ritual	Sabbath rituals
vv. 7–10	**vv. 25–28**			
Then he shall take the two goats and set them before the Lord at the entrance of the tent of meeting. And Aaron shall cast lots over the two goats, one lot for the Lord and the other lot for Azazel. And Aaron shall present the goat on which the lot fell for the Lord and use it as a sin offering, but the goat on which the lot fell for Azazel shall be presented alive before the Lord to make atonement over it, that it may be sent away into the wilderness to Azazel.	And the fat of the sin offering he shall burn on the altar. And he who lets the goat go to Azazel shall wash his clothes and bathe his body in water, and afterward he may come into the camp. And the bull for the sin offering and the goat for the sin offering, whose blood was brought in to make atonement in the Holy Place, shall be carried outside the camp. Their skin and their flesh and their dung shall be burned up with fire. And he who burns them shall wash his clothes and bathe his body in water, and afterward he may come into the camp.			
v. 14				
v. 15				

Animal sacrifices required	Cleansing rituals required	Burnt offerings required	Scapegoat ritual	Sabbath rituals
vv. 18–19 Then he shall go out to the altar that is before the LORD and make atonement for it, and shall take some of the blood of the bull and some of the blood of the goat, and put it on the horns of the altar all around. And he shall sprinkle some of the blood on it with his finger seven times, and cleanse it and consecrate it from the uncleannesses of the people of Israel.				

In order for God's people to experience His mercy, death was required. The Day of Atonement provided a way for their sins to be cleansed through the death of sacrificial animals rather than their own lives. It was a gory, bloody day.

Revisit verses 14–15. Where did the priest place the blood of the sacrificial animals?

What do Hebrews 9:22 and Romans 6:23 teach us about God's forgiveness?

Since the first act of sinful rebellion in the garden of Eden, bloodshed has been required to hold back God's wrath. It's not just the shedding of blood that is needed—otherwise a paper cut might suffice—but rather *death* that is required.

We see it first in Genesis 2:17: "but of the tree of the knowledge of good and evil you shall not eat, for in the day that you eat of it you shall surely die."

What punishment was promised for Adam and Eve's failure to obey God's command?

Sin is more than a mistake. It goes beyond failure and matters more than messing up. Sin is a violation of God's holiness. Sin is serious—*deadly serious*.

If their sins could not be atoned for, the Israelites would die as a result of God's judgment. As we take a hard look at the consequences of sin, we see the same is true for us. I have great hope that this will become your favorite lesson as the Day of Atonement is a truly miraculous gift, but an inescapable part of this day is sitting in the seriousness of our sin and reflecting again on the wonder of God's mercy.

Take a moment to revisit Jonah's prayer found in Jonah 2. Rewrite Jonah's words as if he understood the gravity of his own sin and worshipped as a recipient of extravagant mercy.

BEHIND THE CURTAIN

BIG IDEA: *Christ's death tore the curtain that separated us from the presence of God.*

READ HEBREWS 6:19–20

Several years ago I taught through the Seven Feasts to the women in my church. I wanted to find a way to move our knowledge about the sixth feast from our heads to our hearts, so I got creative.

Our sanctuary includes a large platform with a set of double curtains. We cleared the space, typically filled with instruments and microphones, leaving only an empty void.

As the women read about the Day of Atonement in quiet corners around our church, I extended this invitation:

> "Please leave your belongings here and head into the worship center. Step behind the curtain. As an object lesson, imagine you are entering into the Holy Place, behind the veil. The stakes are still sky high for sin. We still deserve death for our disobedience, but Jesus has taken our punishment. He has already made the sacrifice required for our sin. If you are in Him, you can live in the freedom of forgiveness."

I sat on the front row of the sanctuary as women slipped behind the curtain one by one. There was nothing magical happening. God's Spirit was present on both sides of the curtain, but in studying the Day of Atonement we were reminded of the miracle of God's sacrifice for our sins.

I'm tearing up now as I remember that moment. I'll never get over the honor of watching women get waylaid by the grace of God. As I've written this study, I've earnestly prayed for you to see anew what Christ has done for you and to anchor your life to His redemptive work.

Read and interact with the description of the Most Holy Place within the tabernacle recorded in Exodus 25:10–22.

Underline any references to measurements.

Circle any references to building materials (wood, gold, etc.)

Highlight the specific instructions for the mercy seat.

The mercy seat was to be separated from the rest of the tabernacle by an elaborate curtain (or veil). *Read the instructions for the curtain recorded in Exodus 26:31–35.*

What was the curtain made from?

What image(s) were on the curtain?

How was the curtain hung?

Review Leviticus 16:2. When Aaron was instructed to go "inside the veil" on the Day of Atonement, this was the curtain he passed through.

What did Aaron find behind the curtain?

As the Levitical priests performed the rituals for the Day of Atonement, they were proclaiming the miraculous truth that God would mercifully forgive the sins of His people that year, despite their continued sin. Perhaps on some level they understood the significance of this day. What they could not have known was that they were also foretelling the atoning work of Christ on the cross. *Each year when they entered the holy of holies, the high priest was proclaiming the gospel.*

Read about Christ's death in Matthew 27:45–56. Just like the Day of Atonement we read about in Leviticus 16 and 23, this was a gory, bloody day.

What happened the moment Christ gave up His spirit?

Without the Old Testament, we could not understand that the veil separated God's people from His wrath. Without the New Testament, we'd never know that the veil was torn when Christ was crucified, satisfying God's wrath against our sin. Once again, the Old and New Testaments work together like interlocking pieces of the same puzzle to point us to Jesus and His redemptive work in our lives.

Without both pieces of the puzzle, the image would be incomplete.

While many of the other feasts have a New Testament counterpart (Passover, Pentecost, the Lord's Supper), the Day of Atonement does not. We have no need for a yearly sacrifice for our sins because Jesus paid the penalty required once and for all. Because Christ was the perfect, sinless sacrifice, His death atones not just for a year but once and for all (Heb. 7:27).

The tabernacle, the holy of holies, and the curtain were all pointing forward to the better Day of Atonement that was to come.

Compare Leviticus 23:26–32 and Hebrews 4:14–16 in the chart below by circling the similarities and underlining the contrasts.

Leviticus 23:26–32	Hebrews 4:14–16
"And the LORD spoke to Moses, saying, 'Now on the tenth day of this seventh month is the Day of Atonement. It shall be for you a time of holy convocation, and you shall afflict yourselves and present a food offering to the LORD. And you shall not do any work on that very day, for it is a Day of Atonement, to make atonement for you before the LORD your God. For whoever is not afflicted on that very day shall be cut off from his people. And whoever does any work on that very day, that person I will destroy from among his people. You shall not do any work. It is a statute forever throughout your generations in all your dwelling places. It shall be to you a Sabbath of solemn rest, and you shall afflict yourselves. On the ninth day of the month beginning at evening, from evening to evening shall you keep your Sabbath.'"	"Since then we have a great high priest who has passed through the heavens, Jesus, the Son of God, let us hold fast our confession. For we do not have a high priest who is unable to sympathize with our weaknesses, but one who in every respect has been tempted as we are, yet without sin. Let us then with confidence draw near to the throne of grace, that we may receive mercy and find grace to help in time of need."

Think back, what rituals did the high priest need to complete before entering the Holy Place?

What was on the line if he did not complete the sacrifices and rituals required on the Day of Atonement?

In contrast, what word is used for how we are encouraged to approach the throne of grace?

What caused the shift?

We can come into God's presence with confidence, assured that the work of atonement is already done! Read these amazing words found in Hebrews 10:19–22:

> Therefore, brothers, since we have confidence to enter the holy places by the blood of Jesus, by the new and living way that he opened for us through the curtain, that is, through his flesh, and since we have a great priest over the house of God, let us draw near with a true heart in full assurance of faith, with our hearts sprinkled clean from an evil conscience and our bodies washed with pure water.

My hope is that your study of the Day of Atonement from Leviticus makes this piece of the redemptive puzzle clearer. *How has today's study sharpened your understanding of the truth revealed in Hebrews 10?*

To end today's study, I invite you to go behind the curtain. It doesn't have to be an actual curtain, just find a place, right where you are, to seek the Lord.

Please leave your belongings here and step behind the curtain. As an object lesson, imagine you are entering into the Holy Place, behind the veil. The stakes are still sky high for sin. We still deserve death for our disobedience, but Jesus has taken our punishment. He has already made the sacrifice required for our sin. If you are in Him, you can live in the freedom of forgiveness.

DWELL

BIG IDEA: *We are God's temple. His Spirit lives in us.*

READ EXODUS 25:17-22

Picture it.

Jesus' disciples had just endured the arrest, murder, and burial of their leader and friend. The One they had pledged their lives to had been taken from them in the most violent and jarring way possible. They had barely settled into their grief when Jesus rose from the dead. Suddenly, He was back in their midst. He had told them that all of this would happen, but surely His warnings didn't fully prepare them for the whiplash of being with Jesus, then having Him ripped from them, only to have Him return once again.

Their hearts must have still been tender when Jesus gathered the disciples together again on a mountain. The time had passed for sermons. This was a commissioning service.

> And Jesus came and said to them, "All authority in heaven and on earth has been given to me. Go therefore and make disciples of all nations, baptizing them in the name of the Father and of the Son and of the Holy Spirit, teaching them to observe all that I have commanded you." (Matt. 28:18–20a)

Scripture doesn't record what the disciples were feeling, but I know what I would have felt. "Wait! What? You just got back and now you're sending us out? Can't we stay here? With You? Together?"

When I read these verses, I have sympathetic separation anxiety for the disciples. Surely, anyone who had been with Jesus would be undone by the thought of learning to live without Him.

Jesus comforted His friends with these tender words, "And behold, I am with you always, to the end of the age" (v. 20b). Jesus was offering His permanent presence, a radical gift we cannot fully understand without viewing Christ's words through the lens of the Old Testament.

Numbers 2 records the instructions given to the Israelites for how to set up camp in the wilderness along with the formation they were to use as they marched toward the Promised Land. *Read Numbers 2, and fill in the missing information in the graphics below.*

ISRAEL IN CAMP

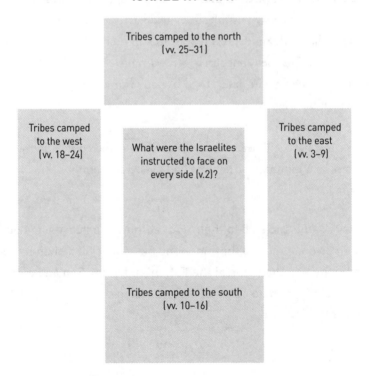

Tribes camped to the north
(vv. 25–31)

Tribes camped to the west
(vv. 18–24)

What were the Israelites instructed to face on every side (v.2)?

Tribes camped to the east
(vv. 3–9)

Tribes camped to the south
(vv. 10–16)

ISRAEL ON THE MARCH

This passage also gives instructions for the formation Israel would use when traveling. *Fill in the prompts in the order listed below to complete the visual for Israel's marching formation.*

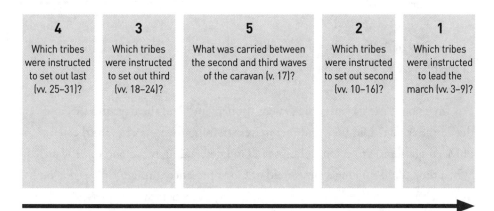

4	3	5	2	1
Which tribes were instructed to set out last (vv. 25–31)?	Which tribes were instructed to set out third (vv. 18–24)?	What was carried between the second and third waves of the caravan (v. 17)?	Which tribes were instructed to set out second (vv. 10–16)?	Which tribes were instructed to lead the march (vv. 3–9)?

What does the placement of the Tent of Meeting (a.k.a. tabernacle) communicate about its importance in the lives of the Israelites?

The mercy seat was contained in the innermost room of the tabernacle. *Revisit Leviticus 16:2. What was so sacred about the mercy seat?*

God taught His people to architect their lives so that His presence was central. Whether their day held rhythms of routine or upheaval, whether standing still or on the move, the Israelites could keep their eyes fixed on the place where God promised to dwell among them on the Day of Atonement. While the presence of God among them must have caused some fear, surely it was also a source of awe and comfort.

On the Day of Atonement, God would dwell with man. The God of the universe! In their very midst!

But what about the day after the Day of Atonement? And the day after that and the day after that? Did they find themselves straining their eyes toward the Tent of Meeting, hoping to catch a glimpse of God descending in a cloud once again? When they could no longer be assured of God's presence through a pillar of cloud by day or a pillar of fire by night (Ex. 13:21–22) . . . when they had to leave Mount Sinai behind after God descended it with thunder, lightning, and the blast of the trumpet, did they miss the presence of God in their midst? I would have!

The miracle of Christ is not just that He atoned for our sins, but that He gifted us His presence in a way that didn't require the mercy seat and the tabernacle.

Let's practice interlocking the puzzle pieces of God's Word once again. *Fill in the words for the following passages.*

ISAIAH 7:14

MATTHEW 1:23

We first read the word "Immanuel" in Isaiah's Old Testament prophecy about the coming Christ. Isaiah repeats this name in 8:8 but does not elaborate on the meaning.

It isn't until we see the name again in the book of Matthew that the impact of Jesus' name is revealed.

The idea of God coming to be with them would not have been foreign to the Israelites. They had seen Him do it. The idea of God coming to *stay* with them, however, would have been revolutionary!

God's all-day, every-day presence is our unique and extraordinary gift as New Testament believers.

The tabernacle described in the Old Testament no longer stands. We don't need it to. *According to 1 Corinthians 3:16, where is the temple now?*

According to Ephesians 2:22, where is the dwelling place of God?

As His beloved children, *we are Christ's temple*. The miracles of the cross go beyond saving us from sin and death and transform us from the inside out. He is with us always, because He dwells inside of us.

When God commissioned Moses to lead the Israelites away from Mount Sinai, Moses agreed, on one condition. *Write down his words recorded in Exodus 33:15.*

The disciples, on the other hand, when they were commissioned to lead God's people in declaring the gospel to the world, had no such condition. They didn't need it. Remind yourself of what Christ told His disciples after He commissioned them to go and tell (Matt. 28:20b). *Write that promise here:*

They didn't have to listen for a trumpet blast.
They didn't have to see God through a cloud.
They didn't have to wait for the Day of Atonement.

God was with them, *inside their hearts,* everywhere they went. And God is with us, *inside our hearts,* everywhere we go.

This changes everything!

Think back to the graphics of the Israelite camp. Is God's constant presence central to your life? Is that the driving force you take with you as you go, wherever you go? It can be.

Fill out the chart again, this time place God in the center, as He is always with you. Use the other boxes to fill out the categories of your life (marriage, parenting, work, friendship, etc.).

God's constant presence serves to remind us of our sin, in the same way God's presence reminded Israel of their need to atone. But it also means we have full and constant access to the comforts of His love, to the power of His Spirit, and to the purity of His righteousness. Jesus dwells inside us by His Spirit now. And He will dwell with us fully one day soon.

End today's study by reflecting on the promise of Revelation 21:3. Write down what life will be like when the dwelling place of God is fully and forever with man (v. 4).

MORE-THAN-ENOUGH GRACE

BIG IDEA: *God's grace is an invitation to stop re-living the Day of Atonement.*

READ EPHESIANS 2:8–9

I have Isaiah 10:1 written on a bright green Post-it note on my desk.

It says, "Woe to those who decree iniquitous decrees, and the writers who keep writing oppression."

As a writer (of Bible studies, no less), this verse gives me a healthy dose of writer's block. It forces me to pause and pray before I write. It's possible that all my well-intentioned words will lead some of you toward greater bondage instead of greater freedom. And, frankly, that's a thought I cannot bear.

Perhaps as you've read about the Day of Atonement, your heart has defaulted to patterns of guilt and fear. When I tell you to embrace rhythms of sitting in your sin, perhaps you hear me saying you should sit in your *shame.* Maybe some of you are like me, driven by achievement and its ugly twin, perfectionism. We don't need reminders to take our sin seriously. We're already thinking about our failures 24-7. The harder pill for us to swallow is the extravagance of God's grace.

Revisit the instructions for the Day of Atonement from Leviticus 23:26–32. Circle the word afflict every time it appears in the text.

Circle all of the words below that are good synonyms for the word afflict.

BURDEN

BOTHER   OPPRESS   GRIEVE

HELP

PUNISH   COMFORT   SUPPORT

ABUSE   HURT   CALM   SOOTHE
           STRIVE   REST

In this case, God's people were to participate in the Day of Atonement with their own discomfort. Two "afflictions" were required:

1. A Food Offering

READ LEVITICUS 23:27

Leviticus 2 gives us an overview of food offerings (also known as grain offerings). List what was included in the food offering in verses 1–2.

A portion of the food offering was dedicated to God and burned on the altar, the other portion was used to feed the Levitical priests.

Why would gifting this food to God be an "affliction?"

2. Sabbath

READ LEVITICUS 23:28, 30–31
Based on what you already know about Sabbath, what was God requiring here?

Why was Sabbath an "affliction"?

Both the giving of an offering and the commitment to stop working on this sacred day were meant as physical expressions to reflect the Israelites' hearts toward God. God didn't need their gifts of grain or their rest. He was asking them to take steps of humility as an outward expression of their inward grief over their sin.

When we struggle to accept God's gift of grace, it may appear we are being humble. In reality, failure to accept that Christ has fully atoned for our sins is a sneaky form of pride. (Gulp!) Before I show you how, let's look again at what the Bible tells us about God's grace.

Just like He did with the Israelites, God used affliction to teach the apostle Paul about grace. Paul prayed that a "thorn in the flesh" would be removed from his life. *Write down the Lord's answer, recorded in 2 Corinthians 12:9.*

What word is used to describe God's grace?

We are the recipients of "sufficient grace." That means we have:

- Plentiful grace . . .
- Abundant grace . . .
- More-than-enough grace . . .

. . . in Christ.

God's contract of grace toward the Israelites in Leviticus had to be renewed each year. Ours has no expiration date.

The sins of your past are covered by grace.
The sins of your present are covered by grace.
The sins of your future? Yep, they're covered by grace. This is not just any grace. It's sufficient grace!

Look again at the words you circled as synonyms for affliction. Now create a list of synonyms for the word sufficient. Here are a few of my favorites to get you started:

Plenteous
Enough
Lots and lots

When we fail to accept that God's grace is enough to cover our sin, we're living in pride because the focus is ultimately on *us*. We're so hyper-attentive to *our* sin, *our* feelings, *our* failures, that we miss that Christ is the one who did the work required for us to be forgiven.

Many of us live as if the Day of Atonement is still in effect. We afflict ourselves with shame, guilt, fear, and dread, hoping and praying our meager offerings will be enough to earn God's acceptance, when He has already given it freely and abolished our need for elaborate rituals with one final Day of Atonement. Hear me, friend. *You're not the one person the cross isn't big enough for.* You are the recipient of sufficient, elaborate, over-the-top, permanent grace.

Write out the passages written on the puzzle pieces below.

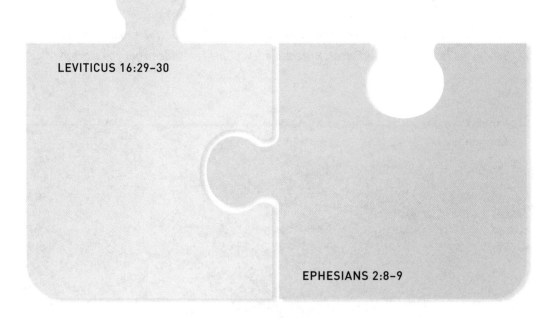

LEVITICUS 16:29–30

EPHESIANS 2:8–9

Rather than thinking of these as contradictory approaches to sin and atonement, consider them interlocking pieces of the same puzzle.

How does Leviticus 16 point forward to Christ?

How does Ephesians 2 point backward to Christ?

Once again, to clearly see God's character and His redemptive plan, we need to look beyond a single piece of the puzzle. As we study the Day of Atonement, our call to action isn't to afflict ourselves because of our sin, but to live as women freed by the overwhelming gift of God's grace.

Circle back once more to Leviticus 23:30. What did God promise for those who did not rest on the Day of Atonement?

God's command to rest was especially severe on this day. We're all tempted to keep working toward salvation. God's command to rest applies to us. Through His promised grace He is saying:

Rest in this.
Rest in this.
REST. IN. THIS!

I don't want to end today's study with another assignment or prompt. It feels contrary to everything we've read in the Bible together today. Instead, I offer an invitation.

For every woman familiar with shame . . .

For each of us frustrated by our chronic failure . . .

For every one of us who cannot fathom God's grace can cover *our* sin . . .

For every time we miss God's mark . . .

For every moment spiritual amnesia wipes our memories of God clean . . .

Our challenge is to stop living as if the Day of Atonement is still required and to fall face-first into God's elaborate grace.

REST IN THIS

BIG IDEA: *Rest in the divine mercy of Jesus.*

READ PSALM 136

I am a delayed processor. The wheels inside my brain are always turning; they just turn slowly. If I had just spent four days studying the mercy of God like you have, my heart would need some time to absorb it. I'd want to soak in the sweetness of God's redemptive work for a while.

And since I started this lesson with an invitation to sit in your sin, I want to end it with an invitation to sit in the gift of God's mercy.

Whether you're a slow processor like me, or you're ready to move on to the next big idea, I hope you will accept my invitation to take today a little slower. Not only does God's Spirit dwell within us, but so can His Word.

That is the promise of Colossians 3:16. *Read and record this precious verse below.*

Just like Christ is with us always, His Word can live inside us with permanence. The Truth doesn't have to come and go, like a cloud. We can hold onto what we've learned this week and God can use it to transform us from the inside out.

I've invited you to rest in the reality of God's grace, but rest is hard and so often does not come easily to us. I can't clear your calendar or tackle your to-do list. I can, however, invite you to spend the next few minutes focused only on God's Word and to allow Truth to settle in and make itself at home. Think of it like a mini-Sabbath, right here in the pages of your Bible study.

Spend your study time today parked in Psalm 136. Jews often refer to this Psalm as "the Great Hallel." Since this Psalm has historically been sung at the conclusion of the Passover meal, many believe these are the words Jesus sang with His disciples at the last supper (Matt. 26:30).

This Psalm proclaims twenty-six acts of kindness God has extended toward His children. It is a poetic and poignant reminder of God's character.

READ PSALM 136

And rest in who He is.
Rest in this.
Rest in this.
Rest. In. This . . .

3 QUESTIONS FOR GROUP STUDY

1. What does this tell us about God?

2. What does this tell us about us?

3. How should we respond?

The Feast of Booths

John 7 records Jesus observing the seventh feast, the Feast of Booths, an eight-day celebration in autumn after harvest during which the Israelites built leafy tents and camped in remembrance of the forty years their ancestors spent wandering.[14] Though this feast has been observed by God's people thousands of times throughout history, this is the one and only time Jesus preached a sermon during the Feast of Booths. The religious leaders were outraged by Jesus' teaching, convinced He had blasphemed God on their holy feast day.

Jesus replied simply, ""My teaching is not mine, but his who sent me" (v. 16).

While the religious leaders were nearly foaming at the mouth because of Jesus' words, Jesus was honoring the spirit of the Feast of Booths, passed down in Leviticus 23.

The final feast was meant to shine the spotlight on God, to remind His children of His character, and to shock our hearts into new rhythms. Begin this week's study by reading Jesus' entire Feast of Booths sermon, found in John 7:14–24. As you do, may you resist your inner Pharisee who wants to make the feasts into a list of do's and don'ts. Instead, remember again why the feasts exist: to remind you of the goodness and mercy of God.

FORGET NOT HIS BENEFITS

BIG IDEA: *Let's review all God has revealed in the first six feasts.*

READ LEVITICUS 23:37–44

I spent my first few years out of college as a high school history teacher. As I was learning the ropes, a wise teaching mentor encouraged this structure for daily curriculum:

> Tell them what you're going to teach them.

> Teach them.

> Tell them what you taught them.

Good teachers know that review needs to be built into the cadence of learning. Since God is the very best teacher, He has filled His Word with constant reminders of the Truth He's trying to show us.

Before Leviticus 23 comes to a close and God stops speaking to Moses about the Seven Feasts, He takes the time for a review. *Record His words from Leviticus 23:37–38.*

God gave the commandments for the first six feasts. As He was outlining the seventh and final feast, He changed the pattern.

Command.
Command.
Command.
Command.
Command.
Command.
Change the pattern: review.

Where have we seen this rhythm before?

This is the same pattern we see at creation (Gen. 1) and throughout the Seven Feasts. God invites us to change the pattern of our lives and then shows us how to do it.

Has this study led to the change of any patterns in your life? Write about that below. If not, ask God to show you if there are any changes that He wants to make in your life.

God summarized the festal calendar as a reminder that the feasts were sacred and set apart. He also reminded the Israelites that they were commanded to participate in honoring Him beyond their regular rhythms of Sabbath and sacrifices through the Seven Feasts. Since the Lord saw fit to take the time to review the big idea, we will too. Let's take a flyover of all we've learned from the first six feasts, assembling some of the picture of God's character as we go.

By practicing seeing the Seven Feasts through a gospel lens, we train ourselves to see all of Scripture the same way. Let's look back at the six Feasts we've already studied.

Feast #1: Passover

Review Leviticus 23:4–5. List how the Israelites were commanded to observe this feast.

Summarize the verses listed in the chart below.

EXODUS 12:5–6	REVELATION 5:12

How does Exodus 12:5–6 point forward to Christ's coming?

How does Revelation 5:12 point backward to Christ's death, burial, and resurrection?

Write your big takeaways on the character of God portrayed in this feast on the puzzle piece.

GOD IS . . .

Feast #2: The Feast of Unleavened Bread

Review Leviticus 23:6–8. List how the Israelites were commanded to observe this feast.

Summarize the verses listed in the chart below.

EXODUS 12:15	1 CORINTHIANS 5:7

How does Exodus 12:15 point forward to Christ's coming?

How does 1 Corinthians 5:7 point backward to Christ's death, burial, and resurrection?

Write your big takeaways on the character of God portrayed in this feast on the puzzle piece.

GOD IS . . .

Feast #3: The Feast of Firstfruits

Review Leviticus 23:9–14. List how the Israelites were commanded to observe this feast.

Summarize the verses listed in the chart below.

LEVITICUS 23:10	1 CORINTHIANS 15:22–23

How does Leviticus 23:10 point forward to Christ's coming?

How does 1 Corinthians 15:22–23 point backward to Christ's death, burial, and resurrection?

Write your big takeaways on the character of God portrayed in this feast on the puzzle piece.

GOD IS . . .

Feast #4: The Feast of Weeks

Review Leviticus 23:15–22. List how the Israelites were commanded to observe this feast.

Summarize the verses listed in the chart below.

JOEL 2:28–29	ACTS 2:4

How does Joel 2:28–29 point forward to the outpouring of the Holy Spirit at Pentecost?

How does Acts 2:4 point backward to Christ's death, burial, and resurrection?

Write your big takeaways on the character of God portrayed in this feast on the puzzle piece.

GOD IS . . .

Feast #5: The Feast of Trumpets

Review Leviticus 23:23–25. List how the Israelites were commanded to observe this feast.

Summarize the verses listed in the chart below.

JOSHUA 6:5	REVELATION 11:15

How does Joshua 6:5 point forward to Christ's coming?

How does Revelation 11:15 point backward to Christ's death, burial, and resurrection?

Write your big takeaways on the character of God portrayed in this feast on the puzzle piece.

GOD IS . . .

Feast #6: The Day of Atonement

Review Leviticus 23:26–32. List how the Israelites were commanded to observe this feast.

Summarize the verses listed in the chart below.

LEVITICUS 16:24	1 JOHN 2:2

How does Leviticus 16:24 point forward to Christ's coming?

How does 1 John 2:2 point backward to Christ's death, burial, and resurrection?

Write your big takeaways on the character of God portrayed in this feast on the puzzle piece.

GOD IS . . .

In a single chapter (23) in a single book (Leviticus) God has revealed much about Himself through the Seven Feasts. If we skip these feasts entirely in our study of God's Word or fail to see them through a redemptive lens, we miss the full picture God paints of Himself through His Word.

Wrap up today's review by reflecting on who God is using the questions below.

What characteristics of God are most evident in the Seven Feasts?

What surprises you about God from the Seven Feasts?

What encourages you about God from the Seven Feasts?

What questions do you have about God from the Seven Feasts?

A MIGHTY FORTRESS

BIG IDEA: *God is our shelter.*

READ PSALM 46:1–3

Of all of the places I can spend my time, I like home best. I know that it isn't always true for all of us all the time, but home is meant to be a haven, a respite from the battles of life. When I step behind my front door, my shoulders relax, my pulse slows, my feet slide easily into the comfy slippers that have conformed to my feet through lots of use. It's my place. My shelter.

How about you? Are you the kind of woman who only comes home to crash or a homebody like me?

I'm always on the go				I wish I was home more				Homebody all the way		
1	2	3	4	5	6	7	8	9	10

In the Feast of Booths, God instructed the Israelites to temporarily forgo the comforts of home. Whether the thought of camping exhilarates you ("Let me show you my zero degree sleeping bag") or terrifies you ("Can I bring my pillow? And my couch? And my cat?"), the heart of this feast is sure to make you feel right at home.

Read the instructions for the Feast of Booths, recorded in Leviticus 23:39–43. Record the details for this feast below.

What date did the feast begin?

How long did the feast last?

What was required on the first day of the feast? What was required the day after the feast (the eighth day)?

This feast was bookended by Sabbath rest. Based on all you've learned about the importance of Sabbath from this study, why do you think God scheduled the final feast this way?

Where were God's people instructed to dwell during this feast?

The meaning of this feast wasn't cryptic. God revealed it plainly. Record the takeaway God intended for His people from the Feast of Booths (v. 43).

Once again, God is combatting His people's spiritual amnesia by reminding them of His faithful care. Let's remind ourselves too.

Why did God's people need to be delivered from Egypt?

What remarkable things did God do to extract His people from Egypt?

For the Israelites, freedom was disorienting. True, they were rescued from the oppression of Pharaoh, but suddenly, everything in their world seemed uncertain. *Use the passages below to record some of the concerns of the Israelites post-rescue.*

Exodus 16:3

Exodus 17:3

Exodus 32:1

When God's people expressed a need, God met that need. Every time. Without fail.

When they were hungry, what did God send (Ex. 16:12)?

When they were thirsty, what did God send (Ex. 17:6)?

When they wanted a great leader, who did God send (Ex. 32:30)?

As they wandered for forty years, homeless, and without a nation or neighborhood to call their own, God met another need. *He* was their shelter, their refuge from the strain of life in an unforgiving desert. Though forced to live without the comforts of home, they were never forced to live without comfort. God, their Comforter, was always with them.

Spiritual amnesia can be triggered by struggle, but it can also kick in in seasons of abundance. Remember, the Seven Feasts were instructions for life in the Promised Land. These feasts were to be observed by God's people when they were settled in the land God had given them instead of while they still wandered. We know from the rest of the Old Testament that God's people put down roots, built homes and cities, and eventually became an established nation that still exists in the Promised Land today. Life spent living in tents in the desert quickly became a distant memory, but the Israelites' need to be sheltered by God never dwindled. The Feast of Booths was an annual, physical reminder that no matter where the Israelites lived, God was their True Shelter.

The concept of "shelter" may not come as naturally to us as it did to the Israelites. Most of us have always had a place to come home to. It's hard for us to grasp the kind of anxiety that accompanies not knowing where you'll sleep at night.

Think of "shelter" like a roof. Under the roof in the graphic below, fill in everything you seek protection from, including physical, emotional, and spiritual threats.

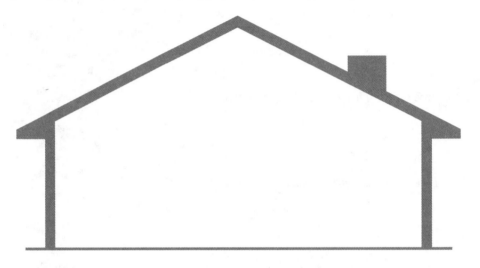

Read the following verses. What does each one teach about shelter?

Psalm 27:5

Psalm 91:1–4

Proverbs 18:10

Though God may gift you with a house for physical protection, friends and family for emotional protection, and a church for spiritual protection, ultimately He is the "roof" over your life, and the only one able to shelter you from the hardships that are an inevitable part of wandering in this "desert" of brokenness.

Reflect back on your life. List any seasons that felt like a desert.

How was God your shelter in each season? What did He protect you from?

So often, we pray for God to give us things like a house . . . a relationship . . . a job. Those things are good and it's okay to ask God for them, but ultimately, what we are asking God for is a refuge from the harsh realities of life. He grants that desire by giving us His presence here on earth. He has also promised a permanent, eternal shelter to come. *Record His promise from John 14:2–3.*

The Feast of Booths was God's plan to remind His people that He is the one who meets their needs. Both in times of plenty and times of desperation, they can run to Him, *we can run to Him,* and find refuge.

My favorite passage about the shelter of God is Psalm 91:4. It's a verse I pray for my sons most days when I drop them off at school, and one I'm stopping to pray for you now as I write these words.

To wrap up today's study, spend time considering this verse, then draw a picture about the kind of shelter God is to His children.

THE GREAT CAMPOUT

BIG IDEA: *God's instructions are rarely comfortable or convenient.*

READ LUKE 9:23–26

It should have been an easy yes.

I was gathered for a ministry summit. The room was filled with like-minded Christ followers who would have celebrated if I'd chosen to obey. I didn't. I chose comfort instead.

The pastor who was leading us had just finished teaching on the cost of following Christ. In a unique approach to a response time, he instructed us to stand, right where we were, and sing the words to "I Have Decided to Follow Jesus," a cappella. At first, no one moved. My heart started to race. My eyes dropped to the floor. I gripped the edge of my chair . . . *What if I'm embarrassed? What if I'm a fake? What if someone laughs at me?*

An inner war was raging between boldly standing for Christ and my own comfort. Comfort took an early lead. I started mumbling the words under my breath, not exactly a bold declaration of faith. I sat in my chair and wrestled unaware that others were wrestling too. No one was singing. Finally, a single voice started singing loud and clear.

"I have decided to follow Jesus . . ."

Another joined.

"I have decided to follow Jesus . . ."

More started singing.

"I have decided to follow Jesus . . ."

It sounded like a choir now.

"No turning back. No turning back."

I did eventually join with the others, but I felt like I had been punched in the gut. If I could not stand for Jesus in a room full of other Christians, how would I ever stand for Him in a world that does not recognize Him?

In that moment, I knew—if I really wanted God to use me, I'd have to surrender my cravings for comfort.

Can you think of a moment in your own life when God wanted to use you as a witness for Him but you chose comfort instead? Write about it below.

Circle back to the Feast of Booths. What unique requirements were given for this feast (Lev. 23:40–43)?

Look again. Who was required to stay in booths (a.k.a. tents)?

We know from Exodus 12:37 that hundreds of thousands of men fled Egypt during the Exodus. Add in women and children, and Israel likely numbered at least two million as they set out for the Promised Land.

In the second year after they fled, Moses took a census of able-bodied men (excluding the Levites). *How many men did Moses count (Num. 1:45–46)?*

Add in women, children, men too old or young to fight and an entire tribe, and Israel was clearly growing.

Fast-forward past an entire generation, and by the time Israel entered the Promised Land, their numbers would have been truly staggering. When you consider the Feast of Booths, don't imagine a few friends gathered around a warm fire. Picture the entire state of Oklahoma camped out for one week of the year and you get a better idea for what this feast was like.

For those of us with small children, the idea of observing this feast is anxiety inducing. The logistics of moving my family to a tent for a week makes me extra grateful to be a New Testament child of God. *Imagine you are an Israelite woman observing this feast. Make a quick list of the preparations that would need to be made.*

God wasn't helping His people experience the great outdoors. He was reminding them of His faithful care; but He was also, once again, teaching them how to live in their Promised Land reality.

Like all humans, the Israelites likely settled into routines of comfort and convenience. The Feast of Booths worked like an annual alarm, alerting their hearts of the need for rhythms of worship. The final feasts nudged them to remember what God had already done and to commit themselves to following Him in the year ahead, even when doing so was uncomfortable.

God calls us to uncomfortable lives too.

Revisit Jesus' words recorded in Luke 9:23–26.

What does Christ ask us to deny?

What does He ask us to take up?

This is the sacred rhythm of being a Christ follower.

We deny our comfort because Christ gave up His comfort for us.

We surrender ourselves and seek to live like our Savior.

We lay down our plans for our lives and live out the lives God calls us to.

I call it the tightrope of terrified obedience. With our eyes fixed on Jesus, we take one uncomfortable step after another as He transforms us into His image. The Bible never calls us to comfortable Christianity, but instead to regular rhythms of sacrifice, surrender, and stretching. Just like the Israelites, I need to be reminded that obeying God will cost me. Why do it? For the same reason the Israelites did when they observed the Feast of Booths. *Because He is worthy.*

He may never require you to pitch a tent of remembrance, but He has certainly called you to embrace the uncomfortable for His name's sake. *Look up the following passages. Next to each one write what God has called you to.*

Romans 12:1–2

Galatians 5:13

Ephesians 2:10

2 Timothy 1:9

1 Peter 2:9

The Feast of Booths was an opportunity for God's people to once again commit to obedience, even when it was costly and inconvenient. As we study this piece of the puzzle, we're reminded that we cannot do what God calls us to if we're unwilling to be uncomfortable.

There will never be an easy time to follow Jesus. Never. Follow Him anyway.

To conclude today's study, pray through the following areas of your life. Ask the Lord to reveal any area where you are unwilling to experience discomfort in order to obey Him.

In my career

In my friendships

In my marriage

With my children

In my church

With my health

With my finances

With my future

With my daily habits

REST AND REMEMBER

BIG IDEA: *Repeat the pattern of the Seven Feasts.*

READ PSALM 46:9, 77:11, 119:55

We all fight constant temptations to prioritize wrongly, spend our time in futility, and cast our crowns at the foot of the wrong thrones. The Bible works like a defibrillator, shocking my heart back into right rhythms again and again. When we read God's Word, our rhythms are reset so that our heart once again beats in step with God's.

As you've studied the Seven Feasts, has God jump-started anything in your heart? Write about it below.

As this study begins to wrap up, you may be wondering what new rhythms Christ is calling you to through His Word. As we consider where we go from here, let's look again at the purpose of God's Word.

Flip all the way back to Day 1 of this study. Record the six rules of Hermeneutics in the blanks below.

Rule #1:_____

Rule #2:_____

Rule #3:_____

Rule #4:_____

Rule #5:_____

Rule #6:_____

Right application of Scripture only flows from a right understanding of who God is. *List the characteristics of God you see displayed in the Seven Feasts.*

The Israelites were commanded to observe the Seven Feasts as a practical way to remember who God is. God graciously structured their calendars in a way that combatted their spiritual amnesia.

Has your own spiritual amnesia been exposed through this study?

What do you tend to forget most often about God?

Look up Matthew 5:17 in several different Bible translations. If you are studying in a group, read the verse aloud from multiple versions.

I appreciate the NLT paraphrase of this verse, "Don't misunderstand why I have come. I did not come to abolish the law of Moses or the writings of the prophets. No, I came to accomplish their purpose."

The words Jesus is referencing here are the very ones we've spent eight weeks studying. Jesus is telling us that His purpose in coming was not to nullify the Old Testament, including the Seven Feasts, but rather to fulfill everything the feasts were designed to teach God's people.

Think about what you've learned in these weeks. How does Jesus fulfill the main idea of the Seven Feasts?

Because of Jesus, we no longer live under the letter of the law. We do still live, however, under the spirit of the law. We're still prone to spiritual amnesia. We still need to rest in God's redemptive plan. Our hearts still need to be shocked back into praise on a regular basis. So, what rhythms can we take away from the Old Testament feasts into our New Testament reality?

We can rest, celebrate, and remember.

LET US REST

Let's head back to the chapter we've visited so often together, Leviticus 23.

Read the entire chapter once again. Write down the reference for every time the word rest *or* Sabbath *is included in the text.*

Let's practice widening the lens. Remember a single chapter of the Bible always reflects the whole Bible. *Look up the following passages. What does each one teach about rest?*

Genesis 2:2–3

Psalm 23:2–3

Matthew 11:28–30

Hebrews 4:9–11

The command to rest is not unique to the experience of the Israelites in the Promised Land. It is a command for all of God's people. God modeled the practice of intentional rest at creation. As His image bearers, we have the opportunity to repeat the pattern by resting regularly. In so doing, we express our faith in God to keep working even when we don't, and we ask Him to refuel and sustain us.

Use the assessment tool below to evaluate your own rhythms of rest.

I HAVE A TIME SET APART WEEKLY TO REST AND RECHARGE.

Yes, absolutely   Room for improvement   Not even close

| 1 | 2 | 3 | 4 | 5 | 6 | 7 | 8 | 9 | 10 |

I SEE REST AS AN ACT OF WORSHIP.

Yes, absolutely   Room for improvement   Not even close

| 1 | 2 | 3 | 4 | 5 | 6 | 7 | 8 | 9 | 10 |

I UNDERSTAND THAT MY FRIENDS AND FAMILY NEED REST AND GIVE THEM GRACE WHEN THEY NEED TO DO LESS.

Yes, absolutely   Room for improvement   Not even close

| 1 | 2 | 3 | 4 | 5 | 6 | 7 | 8 | 9 | 10 |

I UNDERSTAND THAT MY VALUE DOES NOT COME FROM MY PRODUCTIVITY, SO I CAN REST WITHOUT GUILT.

Yes, absolutely   Room for improvement   Not even close

| 1 | 2 | 3 | 4 | 5 | 6 | 7 | 8 | 9 | 10 |

Consider talking to a spouse or close friend about patterns of rest in your life. Here are some questions to get you started.

- Do you see me resting regularly?
- What is the biggest hindrance to rest in my life?
- What specific areas of struggle in my life could be helped by more rest?

As you're looking for ways to adjust your life in response to the Seven Feasts, *start with rest.* Rest is a gift given to us by God to help us remember who is really on the throne and to prepare our bodies, minds, and hearts to remember who God is.

What is one commitment you could make to rest more? (Examples: watch less TV, reduce evening commitments, leave Sunday afternoons unscheduled, take vacations from work).

LET US CELEBRATE

Glance again at Leviticus 23. Write down the reference for every time God's people were commanded to eat.

Without cultural context, it's easy for us to assume the feasts were always serious and somber. But remember, the festal calendar mapped the Israelites' holidays. We celebrate Valentine's Day and St. Patrick's Day, and they celebrated Passover and the Feast of Trumpets. This was a time for gathering with family, repeating traditions year after year, and for eating . . . lots of eating.

I hope you don't have the impression that God is anti-feasting. That couldn't be further from the truth. Many of the most significant events in Scripture occurred around feasting. *Look up the following passages and write down what happened in each scene.*

Esther 7:1–3

Matthew 26:17–30

Revelation 19:6–9

Food is God's idea! He created strawberries and blueberries, grains and grapes, steak and eggs. In commanding His people to feast regularly, He was teaching them the invitation recorded in Psalm 34:8, "Taste and see that the LORD is good! Blessed is the man who takes refuge in him!"

The invitation to gather, to feast, and to celebrate the goodness of God is not limited to the Seven Feasts. *Match the following references with the correct verse.*

Ecclesiastes 3:1–4

Praise the LORD!
Praise God in his sanctuary;
     praise him in his mighty heavens!

Psalm 150:1

So, whether you eat or drink, or whatever you
do, do all to the glory of God.

For everything there is a season, and a time for
     every matter under heaven:
     a time to be born, and a time to die;
     a time to plant, and a time to pluck up what is
          planted;

Philippians 4:4

1 Corinthians 10:31

     a time to kill, and a time to heal;
     a time to break down, and a time to build up;
     a time to weep, and a time to laugh;
     a time to mourn, and a time to dance;

Rejoice in the Lord always; again I will say,
rejoice.

Because God has done great things for us, our lives are to be lived in joyful celebration. That doesn't mean every day is easy or that we plaster fake smiles on our faces. It does mean that we initially take time to celebrate the faithfulness of God. The easiest way is to gather other believers around your table for a feast and acknowledge together that God has given you many reasons to celebrate.

Use the assessment tool below to evaluate your own rhythms of celebration.

I HAVE A HABIT OF REGULARLY GATHERING WITH OTHER CHRISTIANS.

Yes, absolutely   Room for improvement   Not even close

| 1 | 2 | 3 | 4 | 5 | 6 | 7 | 8 | 9 | 10 |

HOLIDAYS IN MY HOME ARE CHRIST-FOCUSED.

Yes, absolutely   Room for improvement   Not even close

1 2 3 4 5 6 7 8 9 10

I HAVE JOY.

Yes, absolutely   Room for improvement   Not even close

1 2 3 4 5 6 7 8 9 10

I REFLECT ON WHAT GOD HAS DONE AS OFTEN AS I THINK ABOUT WHAT I WANT HIM TO DO.

Yes, absolutely   Room for improvement   Not even close

1 2 3 4 5 6 7 8 9 10

As you are looking for ways to adjust based on what you've learned from the Seven Feasts, consider re-evaluating your celebrations. *What is one holiday you can focus on this year to adjust your traditions to be more celebratory of God's gifts? Write your ideas below.*

LET US REMEMBER

Record Deuteronomy 6:12 below.

Widen the lens. Who were these words written to?

Circle back to verses 4–8 in Deuteronomy 6. What instructions preceded the invitation to remember?

Through Moses, God handed down the greatest commandment (v. 8) and then instructed His people to repeat God's commands to each other everywhere they went. That's the backdrop for the warning to "take care lest you forget the Lord."

This reminder came:

After God's people had been miraculously emancipated in Egypt.

After they walked across the Red Sea on dry ground.

After God led them by a pillar of cloud by day and a pillar of fire by night.

After they saw the presence of God descend on Mount Sinai.

After God wrote the Ten Commandments on tablets of stone with His own hand.

And yet, their tendency to forget God remained. As does ours. This side of heaven, we will always have to fight against our chronic spiritual amnesia.

God's warning through Moses is the foundation of the Seven Feasts: "take care lest you forget the Lord." Shouldn't it also be the foundation of our lives?

Use the assessment tool below to evaluate your own rhythms of remembrance.

I READ GOD'S WORD DAILY.

Yes, absolutely   Room for improvement   Not even close

1   2   3   4   5   6   7   8   9   10

I ATTEND CHURCH WEEKLY.

Yes, absolutely   Room for improvement   Not even close

1   2   3   4   5   6   7   8   9   10

I OFTEN SPEND TIME WITH CHRISTIAN FRIENDS WHO REMIND ME WHO GOD IS.

Yes, absolutely   Room for improvement   Not even close

1   2   3   4   5   6   7   8   9   10

MY PRAYERS INCLUDE PRAISE FOR THE CHARACTER OF GOD.

Yes, absolutely   Room for improvement   Not even close

1   2   3   4   5   6   7   8   9   10

We are wise to repeat the pattern the feasts establish.

Rest.
Celebrate.
Remember.
Repeat.
Repeat.
Repeat.

Before you start re-arranging your calendar or throwing out your holiday decorations, remember that God's doesn't invite us to a life in the flesh, regulated by rules and requirements. Instead, He invites us to life in the Spirit that flows from listening closely to the sound of His voice.

I don't want you to end this study with a new to-do list or feelings of shame for the areas where your life doesn't reflect the spirit of the Seven Feasts. Instead, I want you to find peace in God's invitation to you to rest, to celebrate, and to remember who He is.

End today's study in prayer, asking God to help you adjust your rhythms to worship Him more and more.

MINING FOR TREASURE

BIG IDEA: *God's Word is a gold mine.*

READ PSALM 119

As I wrote this study, I thought of you often. I wondered . . .

- Is she doing this study alone or in a group?
- What surprised her from God's Word in this study?
- What work did God do in her heart?

If I could, I'd bring every single reader to the farm. We'd have a hay ride and hot apple cider, and we'd sit in a circle and gush about the treasure of God's Word. Then I would look every one of you in the eye and simply say this . . .

Open your Bible again.

Today and tomorrow and next week and next year. Open your Bible again and again. There's gold in them thar' hills!

Today, we will shift away from the Seven Feasts and focus instead on Psalm 119. Psalm 119 is the longest chapter in the Bible, longer than many entire books of the Bible. It is dedicated to a singular topic: the treasure of God's Word. Let's walk through parts of this Psalm together.

God's Word certainly raises a high bar. It was Jesus Himself who said, "You therefore must be perfect, as your heavenly Father is perfect" (Matt. 5:48).

Here, the psalmist reminds us of the extreme elevation of God's standards.

Revisit verse 1. Who does the psalmist declare to be blessed?

Those whose way is _____ and those who _____ in the _____ of the _____.

Circle back to verses 2 and 3. Who does the psalmist promise will be blessed in these verses?

Which of these phrases always applies to you? (Circle all that apply).

I am blameless.

I keep His testimonies.

I seek God wholeheartedly.

I always walk in His ways.

I do no wrong.

I diligently keep God's Word.

Wish there were more circles on your list? Me too.

Until Christ comes, we will remain broken people, in broken bodies, existing in a broken culture, unable to obtain the perfect holiness God calls us to. None of us can honestly declare, "I've done no wrong," or walk perfectly in obedience to Christ.

It is the reality of this bad news that whets our appetite for the good news.

Underline Psalm 119:5 in your Bible.

Aware of his shortfalls, the psalmist cries out to God for help. We cannot be faithful to God's Word on our own; we need the Spirit's help to steadfastly live the life Christ has called us to.

READ PSALM 119:17–24

How would you describe your enthusiasm for God's Word in this season?

What circumstances tugged at the affections of the psalmist?

In your own life, what tends to pull your heart away from wonder-filled devotion to God's Word?

These verses from Psalm 119 give us just a taste of why the Bible is so good for us. *Write out each benefit described in the verses below.*

Psalm 119:9

Psalm 119:26

Psalm 119:47

Psalm 119:93

Psalm 119:105

Psalm 119:39 contains a simple and powerful declaration: "your rules are good." The Bible is not a laundry list of tedious to-dos meant to squash us. Instead, God's Word is good for us because God is so good to us.

When we remember God's law is good, we move from avoidance to eager consumption.

Life is a battle. The psalmist knew this well. *Write down the challenges he recorded in verses 49–56.*

What other challenges has he addressed throughout this psalm?

These words likely weren't written from a place of ease, where time, energy, and resources were abundant and studying God's Word was easy. This was war. There were enemies afoot. Desperation was in the air.

And yet. . . .

"Your statutes have been my songs in the house of my sojourning" (v. 54).

We live in the in between: between Christ's victory and promised return. In many ways, we're still wandering, just like the Israelites who first heard about the feasts on their way to the Promised Land. And yet, God's Word is our tether. The Bible keeps our hearts closely tied to the Lord.

As our time together comes to a close, I want to take this last opportunity to remind you that God's Word is an indescribable gift. Close the book on this study, but never on God's Word.

Open your Bible again tomorrow . . .
And the next day . . .
And the next day . . .

Never stop opening it, until you are united with Christ.

Until that glorious day, when we shall see Christ face to face, let's keep putting the puzzle together, one verse at a time.

NOTES

1. Robert Robinson, "Come, Thou Fount of Every Blessing," 1758, alt. Martin Madan, 1760, from *The Psalter Hymnal*, 1987, Hymnary.org, https://hymnary.org/text/come_thou_fount_of_every_blessing.

2. Dan Graves, "Did Robert Robinson Wander as He Feared?," Christianity.com, April 28, 2010, https://www.christianity.com/church/church-history/timeline/1701-1800/did-robert-robinson-wander-as-he-feared-11630313.html.

3. Personal interview with Rabbi Lane Steinger, Sir Hadash, June 25, 2019. All references to Rabbi Lane throughout the study are from that interview, as well as from follow-up email communications.

4. Charles Foster Kent, "The Development of the Earlier Old Testament Laws," in *The Origin and Permanent Value of the Old Testament* (New York: Charles Scribner's Sons, 1914), 126, Bible Hub, https://biblehub.com/library/kent/the_origin_and_permanent_value_of_the_old_testament/viii_the_development_of_the.htm.

5. Sean Robinson, "She Vanished Years Ago and Famously Reappeared With Amnesia. Inside the Mystery of Jody Roberts," *The News Tribune*, August 17, 2017, https://www.thenewstribune.com/news/local/crime/article167733012.html.

6. "Dissociative Amnesia," Cleveland Clinic, May 20, 2016, https://my.clevelandclinic.org/health/diseases/9789-dissociative-amnesia.

7. Email message from Rabbi Lane to author August 15, 2019.

8. Zola Levitt, *The Seven Feasts of Israel* (Dallas: Zola Levitt, 1979), 3.

9. Personal interview with Rabbi Lane Steinger, Sir Hadash, June 25, 2019.

10. John Piper, "Jesus Came Not to Give Bread but to Be Bread," Desiring God, November 19, 2009, https://www.desiringgod.org/messages/jesus-came-not-to-give-bread-but-to-be-bread.

11. Margaret Matray, "Newcastle Woman Maintains 122-Year-Old Sourdough Starter," *Casper Star Tribune*, December 4, 2011, https://trib.com/news/state-and-regional/newcastle-woman-maintains--year-old-sourdough-starter/article_000fcb17-5a5a-5590-84c2-3b55bb1d80fa.html.

12. Knowles Shaw, "Bringing in the Sheaves,"1974. Noted music.

13. *ESV Study Bible*, Crossway Bibles, 401.

14. John F. Hart, "John," in *The Moody Bible Commentary*, gen. eds. Michael Rydelnik and Michael G. Vanlaningham (Chicago: Moody, 2014), 1672.

Bible Studies for Women

IN-DEPTH. CHRIST-CENTERED. REAL IMPACT.

KEEPING THE FAITH
978-0-8024-1931-6

AN UNEXPLAINABLE LIFE
978-0-8024-1473-1

THE UNEXPLAINABLE CHURCH
978-0-8024-1742-8

UNEXPLAINABLE JESUS
978-0-8024-1909-5

HIS LAST WORDS
978-0-8024-1467-0

I AM FOUND
978-0-8024-1468-7

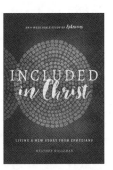

INCLUDED IN CHRIST
978-0-8024-1591-2

THIS I KNOW
978-0-8024-1596-7

WHO DO YOU SAY THAT I AM?
978-0-8024-1550-9

HE IS ENOUGH
978-0-8024-1686-5

IF GOD IS FOR US
978-0-8024-1713-8

ON BENDED KNEE
978-0-8024-1919-4

MOODY Publishers®

From the Word to Life®

Explore our Bible studies at
moodypublisherswomen.com

Also available as eBooks

Where are you in the motherhood journey?

Beauty is one ugly subject!

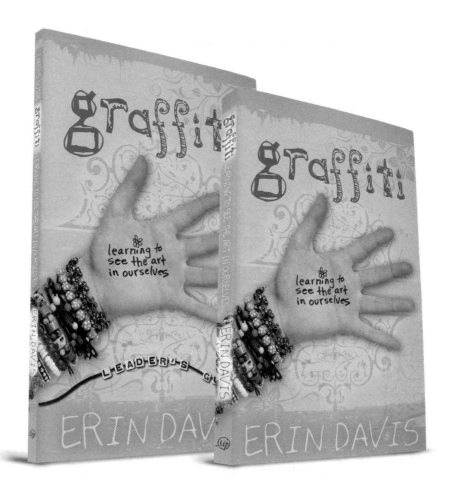

In *Graffiti: Learning to See the Art in Ourselves*, Erin Davis applies what God's Word says about identity, beauty, and worth to the lives of contemporary young women. In fact, women who have never adequately dealt with this issue will find themselves redirecting their spiritual eyes. Don't miss the Leader's Guide, which provides small group leaders with ideas for going deeper.

BOOK 978-0-8024-4585-8 | also available as an eBook
LEADER'S GUIDE 978-0-8024-4586-5 | also available as an eBook